Insider Guide

5/05

Job Hunting A to Z: Landing the Job You Want

2nd Edition

D1567742

Helping you make smarter career decisions.

WetFeet, Inc.

The Folger Building

101 Howard Street

Suite 300

San Francisco, CA 94105

Phone: (415) 284-7900 or 1-800-926-4JOB

Fax: (415) 284-7910

Website: www.WetFeet.com

Job Hunting A to Z: Landing the Job You Want

By Robert A. Fish

ISBN: 1-58207-427-5

Table of Contents

Job Hunting at a Glance

Networking Basics

- Everyone networks.

- It's a valuable skill for many business purposes.

- You can do it engagingly and unobtrusively.

- The information or referral meeting provides a structure.

- The two-minute presentation is a key building block.

- Pursue leads systematically to obtain more meetings.

- Good follow-up is as important as good meetings.

How Networking Leads to Interviews

- Information meetings produce door-opening referrals.

- Well-conducted information meetings often turn into interviews.

- Casual and formal meetings provide insights that will aid you in interviews.

- You will get results if you keep following up with your contacts.

Why Preparation Is Essential

- Everyone involved in the process has particular interests and needs.

- Most interview questions are predictable—plan your answers to highlight your strong points.

- With a prepared presentation, you can take control of the interview.

- A portfolio gives visual weight to your qualifications.

- When you're prepared, you're confident.

Getting the Best Offer

- Learn to recognize the four stages of negotiation.
- You have the most influence in the first three stages.
- Carefully consider your priorities.
- Negotiate with the right person.
- The first person to name numbers is at a disadvantage.
- A successful negotiation leaves both parties satisfied.
- Get the results in writing.

Getting Started

- Overview

- The Bottom Line

- Inside the Hiring Process

- Everyone Networks

- What Interviewing Accomplishes

- A Wider View of Negotiation

Overview

You're eager to get moving with your job campaign. You've put a lot of work into your resume, you're finally satisfied with it, and you're ready to take on the world. You've spoken with friends and obtained some contacts. You know you need to set up meetings with these referrals, and you know how to approach them with letters and phone calls that won't be ignored.

Now's the time to take action—to reach out to your contacts, build on their knowledge and contacts, and discover where the opportunities are. This process is known as *networking*. By tapping into other peoples' stores of insider knowledge as well as their business and social circles, you'll not only learn more than you could at the library and on the Internet, but you'll also find out about job opportunities that never make it to classified ads, job listings, or placement offices.

Still, the very idea of networking makes many people squeamish, and it certainly can be done poorly. The first aim of this Insider Guide is to show you how to network productively, in a way that will make people want to help you. The second is to give you strategies for coming out on top in the often bewildering and intimidating process that results from successful networking—that is, interviewing.

This guide will help you understand the purposes of the various people who may be interviewing you, and will give you step-by-step instructions on preparing for, handling, and following up on interviews. We'll walk you through behavioral, case, stress, and other types of interviews and suggest the best (and worst) ways of answering the most common interview questions—including those designed to trip you up. We'll also describe some strange situations that job seekers before you have faced and cover ways to act gracefully should any of them happen to you.

When an organization is interested in hiring you, preparation is key. The last section of this guide explains the stages of the negotiating process, identifies those in which you can have the most influence, and provides a model for ranking your priorities.

The essential strategies for conducting a successful job search, from start to finish, are all right here. Practice them, and you'll be yards ahead of your competition in the job market.

The Bottom Line

It's a common refrain, and it's true: Most of the best jobs are never advertised—anywhere.

From an organization's point of view, it's easy enough to judge from your resume whether you have the requisite education and experience under your belt. But it's not so easy to discern the other qualities that matter on the job, such as how motivated you are to do the work, how you handle crisis situations, how well you get along well with other employees, how you respond to various types of managers, and how you deal with opportunities and disappointments. That's why most organizations look first at people they know and people who are recommended by people they know when it's time to hire someone. And that's why you need to learn to network.

Still, having an "in" usually isn't enough to land the job. You need to present yourself to your best advantage, in interviews with your would-be supervisor, that person's supervisor, and other members of the team. Preparation based on in-depth knowledge of the interviewing process will help you do that and allow you to walk into interviews confident and relaxed. Finally, when you get a job offer, you want to make sure it reflects your full value to the organization.

Networking, interviewing, and negotiating are the key steps in securing your ideal job—learn to do them well, and you've got a foothold on a brilliant career.

Inside the Hiring Process

Picture the hiring process as a clock. At 1 o'clock everything seems to be humming along fine in the organization. But perfect conditions don't last long in the real world. By 2 o'clock the organization is beginning to perceive that it has some problems. Work is piling up on someone's desk. Customers are complaining about slow response time. Competitors are taking advantage of opportunities the organization can't handle quickly enough. Sales aren't what they need to be to keep production fully occupied. You get the idea.

At 3 o'clock suggestions come up at a staff meeting: "Maybe we need extra help in customer service. Or maybe we need to hire a person with expertise in project management, data analysis, or sales support. Or maybe we can contract out some of the work." But nothing is resolved.

By 4 o'clock the need has become so obvious that a committee is appointed to define what kind of help is really required. It takes until 5 o'clock to come up with job specifications and get the money approved. Key staff people are asked

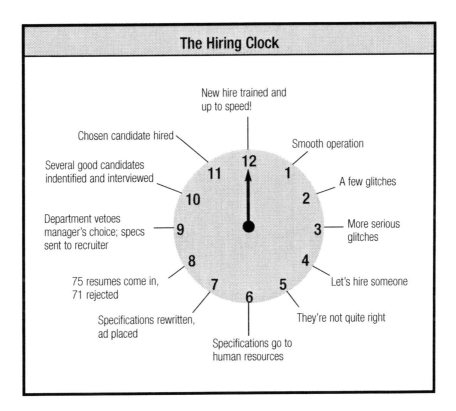

The Hiring Clock

New hire trained and up to speed!

Chosen candidate hired

Several good candidates indentified and interviewed

Department vetoes manager's choice; specs sent to recruiter

75 resumes come in, 71 rejected

Specifications rewritten, ad placed

Specifications go to human resources

They're not quite right

Let's hire someone

More serious glitches

A few glitches

Smooth operation

if they know anyone who might be suitable, and a few names are put forth for consideration. Informal interviewing begins. No one seems right for the job, however, except one person who seems happy where she is.

Now it's 6 o'clock, and the job specifications are sent to human resources. HR spends some time reviewing its files of resumes, asks more questions, and by 7 o'clock has finally developed a classified ad or given the job specifications to a campus placement office. Quite a few resumes come in, but it takes until 8 o'clock to identify a few candidates who seem strong enough to be called in for interviews with the hiring manager.

Getting Started

By 9 o'clock it's clear that none of the four candidates selected is exactly what the hiring manager had in mind—except one, who doesn't meet the approval of the rest of the department. So the job specifications are sent to a recruiter, who produces some better-qualified candidates. Now it's 10 o'clock, but it takes until 11 o'clock to conduct interviews, make the choice, negotiate terms, and get the person started. At midnight, the new hire is up to speed and productive. Then the cycle starts again.

Get in Early

Where do you fit into the process? If you respond to an ad in a newspaper or on the Internet, or your online resume gets matched to the employer's specifications, you're entering the hiring process late in the day, say between 7 and 11 o'clock. At this point, you know for sure that there is a position the employer needs to fill, but you are also up against a lot of competition, which reduces your likelihood of being selected, as well as your bargaining power.

If you can get in earlier, say at 4 or 5 o'clock, when the precise need and job specifications are still being developed, you will encounter far less competition and have a better chance of influencing the employer's thinking to your benefit. Networking is how you gain this advantage. By working through your contacts, you learn of employers' needs before they reach the wider market. You also get the opportunity to propose ways in which you could help fill those needs. The employer gains by making an early selection; you gain by being in a class by yourself.

Everyone Networks

Networking comes naturally to almost all of us. We network when we ask a friend's opinion of a movie. We network when we seek recommendations for good doctors. We network when we try to line up cheap or free lodgings for a trip to Europe. And if the friends we ask can't tell us what we want to know, they often know someone who can. So why not network to learn about career fields, companies, and job opportunities?

Networking can accomplish four important things:

1. It can give you information that will help you direct your efforts more productively and present yourself better.

2. It can garner introductions to people who may control job opportunities.

3. It can let you in on these opportunities earlier in the cycle, giving you a competitive advantage.

4. Finally, the networking process itself adds to your credibility, since the person who refers you is adding his or her favorable judgment to your qualifications.

While you certainly want to take advantage of on-campus interviews and Internet job services, you should also use networking to broaden and improve your opportunities.

What Interviewing Accomplishes

Generally speaking, employers need to know three key things about you:

1. Are you capable of doing the job? Do you have the necessary skills and experience, or can you be readily trained?

2. Are you motivated to do the job? Will you take the trouble to do the job well, ask for guidance when appropriate, and make the necessary effort to meet tight deadlines? Or will you resort to excuses?

3. Are you a person they'll like working with? Will you be a team player and adapt easily to the company culture? Will you be an optimist or a pessimist? Will you give or grab credit?

Resumes provide few answers to the second and third questions and alone are not sufficient to speak to the first. The interview process is intended to help fill in these blanks.

Interviewing potential employees is an art. Some people have a talent for it; others don't. Regardless, it's important that you be well prepared, make the process easier for the interviewer, and realize that the interviewer is trying to find out (whether they do it smoothly or awkwardly) what is not on your resume— namely, how you will behave on the job.

But interviewing is not merely a matter of satisfying interviewers. You also want to determine whether this is the right company, the right job, and the right team for you. After all, you will be committing the majority of your waking hours to the job for a year or 2, if not longer. Ideally, you want to find the work satisfying, enjoy your colleagues, learn a lot, and position yourself to achieve your long-term career goals.

A Wider View of Negotiation

Many people see negotiation as a process of each party trying to get the most for what they have to give. And that's a reasonable way to look at it when you're buying or selling a car, a computer, or a carpet. It's tempting to look at job negotiations in the same way—but not advisable. When you're negotiating an employment contract, you're negotiating the basis for a relationship, and you want to live happily together. This doesn't mean that you have to arrive at a compromise, but that you should come to an agreement that both parties feel is fair.

There are at least four factors that can increase your perceived worth. All of them fit into the context of networking and interviewing, and all of them can be turned to your advantage without alienating potential employers.

1. **How you see and present yourself.** Are you confident? Do you speak convincingly about your accomplishments? Do you have a clear and credible objective? Do you understand and seem to fit in with the company's culture? You will generate more buyer enthusiasm if the company sees you as a long-term asset than if it sees you only as right for this particular job.

2. **How the company values the work to be done.** This is your opportunity to put the work in a broader context than the company may have. Instead of talking about providing good customer service, for example, you might discuss retaining valued customers and increasing business activity. If you present some convincing illustrations, the job might seem worthy of a higher valuation—including, perhaps, a bonus for achieving objectives that you help define.

3. **The company's perception of your appropriateness for the position.** You want to demonstrate that what you've learned and achieved in the past, along with your understanding of the company's needs, makes you more qualified than other candidates.

4. **Your direct discussion of compensation, bonuses, commissions, and other benefits.** This last factor is often thought of as the whole of negotiation. Your attention to the first three factors, however, should already have raised the company's estimation of your value. The direct discussion is where you apply your skills at recapitulation, listening, and politely asserting the value you have established.

Successful Networking

- The Importance of Networking

- Approach Letters

- The Information and Referral Meeting

- Preparing Your Brief Presentation

- When Information Meetings Turn Into Interviews

- Following Up After Meetings

- Networking Dos and Don'ts

The Importance of Networking

Companies tend to recognize that they need to hire someone long before they create a formal job specification and resort to classified ads, the Internet, or a recruiter to bring in candidates. During this gestation period, they often cast about informally to see if anyone within the organization knows of a talented person who might be available. They may consult advisors, vendors, or customers. And they will be more open than usual to discussions with those who present themselves on their own—or better yet, come with an introduction from someone the hiring manager respects.

As it is, organizations themselves engage in networking when they need new employees. Your aim should be to make sure that their networks intersect the network you create.

Why is networking such an important part of a job search? Consider the standard employment resources. Jobs posted on the Internet or advertised in the newspaper and even those listed with campus recruiters may have been difficult for the organization to fill through networking because they are undesirable in some way. And as we've already pointed out, they will certainly put you in competition with many (often 100 or more) other candidates. Often these positions have been filled or are close to being so by the time you become aware of them. Networking, in contrast, gives you an earlier look at an opportunity, at a time when you can still help shape the job description and influence the level and pay range of the position. You will face less competition because no more than a handful of other people will typically be brought in through an organization's own networking activities. And most of these other candidates will already be employed elsewhere and will not have taken the time to prepare as thoroughly as you.

Networking also gets you access to people who might not be responsive to a direct approach letter and provides you with the added advantage of a recommendation from someone the hiring manager knows. Professional career consultants say that a job seeker's chances of obtaining a meeting with a particular individual improve significantly when a good approach letter is coupled with a respected referral. A company's current employees are among the best sources for referrals—many firms report that 40 to 50 percent of open positions are filled with candidates referred by staff members. Moreover, companies view such candidates more favorably than those brought in through other methods, because they already know something about the organization and have a personal connection to it.

Finally, networking may be the only way to locate good opportunities for job seekers whose skills are not in high demand. Even those whose skills are in high demand can benefit from networking, as multiple opportunities and personal referrals will enhance your bargaining position.

Networking Resources

You can start your networking with people you already know. You shouldn't expect them to point you to specific jobs, but they can comment on your resume, how you describe yourself, your career plans, and your talents. Discussing such topics with friends and relatives may lead you to intriguing areas you've never thought to explore. And these people have friends and relatives of their own who could turn out to be valuable resources.

We'll call the people you already know and their connections your **A group**. During this initial round of meetings, you will ask about and get referrals to people your contacts think will be relevant resources for you, such as professionals working in your field of interest or people who work for organizations that interest you.

These people, your **B group**, may or may not know of any specific job opportunities, but they can provide valuable information about current needs in your field, where your skills might fit, what you should emphasize in your presentations, what you need to learn, and resources you can access. The B contacts, if duly impressed, can also introduce you to other B contacts and possibly to people in the C group.

The **C group** consists of people who could hire you if a need exists and you seem to be qualified. While there may not be an immediate opening for you, a well-conducted information and referral meeting with a C person might lead to an interview a month or two later, as well as to introductions to other B and C contacts.

While a telephone call will usually suffice to set up a meeting with an A group person, an approach letter, followed by a phone call to set up an appointment, is usually a more effective and appropriate means of contacting a B or C group person.

ABCs of Networking

The people in your A group might include:

- Friends

- Relatives

- Friends' and relatives' friends and relatives

- Alumni of your college who work in your area of interest or who have participated in the same extracurricular activities as you

- Professors

- Professionals (lawyers, doctors, architects, etc.) you have come to know

- Neighbors, past and present

- Former coworkers

- Anyone you think might be interested in something you've done, such as volunteer work or research

Your B group contacts might include:

- Professionals in your field of interest
- People who know people or organizations in your field of interest
- People employed at organizations where you might like to work, or at similar organizations
- Consultants, entrepreneurs, authors, and other experts in your field of interest

A Taste of Networking

Here are some typical examples of how networking can power your job search if you know how to discuss your background and aspirations—as well as how you would like your contact to help you—in a way that is interesting, credible, and reasonable.

Your meeting with your roommate's brother (an A contact) at graduation leads to an introduction to his tennis adversary, who is a partner in one of the major advertising agencies in Atlanta (a B contact). Your discussion with him in turn leads to an introduction to the director of industry marketing at Delta Air Lines, one of the ad agency's clients (a C contact). Through him you find out about a good job opportunity, which you explore.

You get into a conversation with your hair stylist (A contact) and find out that one of his clients (B contact) is married to a woman who heads your state's Planned Parenthood (a C contact). Although you doubt you want to pursue a career in nonprofit work, a meeting with this woman leads you to reconsider and interview for a position with her organization.

Your meeting with your Aunt Susan (A contact) leads to an introduction to her architect friend Lee (B contact), who is designing a summer home for the CEO of company XYZ (another B contact). When you meet Lee, you mention your interest in market research, which leads to an arranged introduction to his client when the CEO visits the construction site. The CEO is relaxed on this occasion and readily agrees to discuss his plans for XYZ and to introduce you to the head of marketing (C contact). This results in a series of interviews and eventually a job offer, which you negotiate and finally accept.

Approach Letters

The time has come to get down to the business of writing an approach letter. Approach letters, together with approach phone calls, are the means by which you gain access to job opportunities.

Selecting Your Target

It obviously helps in drafting your letter to know to whom it will be sent. Let's say you have learned of a company or organization that interests you. Ideally, you will do some research—learn the products or services the company provides, study the business condition and key issues, and talk with one or more people who work there or have other reasons to know the organization. If WetFeet publishes an Insider Guide on the company, this will be a good investment. This research should provide you with a solid foundation for building an effective communication campaign, such as:

- A fairly clear idea of where your talents might fit within the organization
- Enough knowledge of the company culture to guide how you describe yourself and your interests

- One or more names of senior people to whom you might address your letters, along with some information about their history, interests, and accomplishments. (Don't be afraid to reach high. Senior people often need staff assistance—a great learning opportunity and preparation for future management responsibility, provided the person is a good mentor.)

- And, if you are lucky, an introduction to the person or people who head up the functional areas in which you have an interest

If you've done this research and come up with names of senior managers and functional heads—or better yet, introductions—these are the people to write to first. If, however, you can't acquire names or you've already written to those people and not achieved your goal, then it makes sense to address a letter to the head of human resources, whose name (correctly spelled) and exact title should be available from the switchboard operator. If the switchboard operator can't provide this name, ask for someone in the HR department.

One reason we recommend starting with senior managers and functional heads before writing to human resources is that the hiring managers will know of situations, needs, and future intentions that have not crystallized enough to take the form of a job requisition that human resources would know about. HR managers will almost never hire you for a job that doesn't already exist.

Another reason for dealing with hiring managers first is that HR departments in most companies tend to send you only to interviews for which you are fully qualified by your past experience. This means that HR may rate you below your level of interest and capability—in contrast to a manager who may be more receptive to finding the right person regardless of the little boxes she can check off by a review of your resume, letting the person learn by taking on challenges.

Objectives of the Approach Letter

The objective of an approach letter to a senior manager or head of a functional area is simple: to secure a meeting with the person to whom the letter is addressed or with a hiring manager in the person's organization who would be even more appropriate for you to see. The hiring manager is the person to whom you would report, the person who makes the decision and who has the money to spend. The hiring manager is not the HR person, except in the case of HR positions.

The objective of a letter sent to HR, on the other hand, is to be invited in for a screening interview, which may then lead to interviews with an appropriate hiring manager who has an open job requisition.

You may achieve part of your objective if the person agrees to hold a discussion with you by phone (especially if you live in different cities) but this is not normally as desirable as a face-to-face meeting.

There will likely be a variety of purposes to the meetings you seek during the course of your job search. You may be gathering information and seeking referrals; you may be looking for help in getting introductions within a particular company; or you may be seeking an interview for a position with the person you are targeting. Perhaps you are not sure which is your true purpose, because you have no idea when you write whether you would like to work for the person targeted or even whether you would be suited to do the work the person might have for you.

Fortunately, you don't have to know. Your initial meeting is intended for both you and the other party to get to know each other, exchange information, and test the possibilities. If you restrict its purpose to a job interview, you rule out all other reasons for meeting and actually reduce your chances of gaining an interview—even when such an interview would be appropriate.

It is easier to obtain a meeting for purposes of obtaining advice, information, and possible referrals than it is to obtain an interview. Moreover, an information/referral meeting does not prevent you from receiving any of the potential benefits you would receive from a job interview.

This is because your information/referral meeting gives you every opportunity to demonstrate your experience, your thinking, and the personal qualities that might make you a desirable candidate. Better yet, it allows the interviewer to come up with the idea that you would be an attractive candidate for the current or upcoming position or even a new position created just for you. If your information/referral meeting occurs early enough, when the organization is still in the process of defining its needs, the hiring manager who finds you an attractive candidate may even revise the definition of the position to fit your talents and interests.

Think Information, Not Jobs!

In most cases, an information and referral meeting also serves your purposes better than an interview would, for a number of reasons:

- It's less formal than an interview, so both you and the person you are meeting with will feel free to have a conversation rather than a cross-examination.

- You define the agenda, so you can learn about the broad issues and needs of the person's organization. This will help you discover opportunities still in the making—as well as those that are already defined.

- If you do not identify any opportunities with the organization, you can still obtain referrals to other potentially helpful sources of jobs and advice— unlikely in an interview situation.

- If your contact's organization does have an opening, and you create a favorable impression during this meeting, you will enter the interview process with a considerable advantage.

- If the person you are meeting with has the ability to hire or recommend you, the information meeting format gives you a better opportunity to stimulate interest than a formal interview would. You can easily arrange follow-up meetings or interviews in which the information you have gained can be put to good use.

Don't Include Your Resume

You've gone to a great deal of trouble to prepare a resume for the purpose of campus interviews, so the temptation is strong to attach it to the letter you are going to write. This would simplify life considerably, as all you might then need to write would be a short cover letter. You might come up with something like the following letter from John K. Terkel.

 Example of a Feeble Cover Letter

April 1, 200–

Dear Mr. Matthews,
I would very much like to work for Pepsi Cola in the marketing or sales departments and am well qualified to do so. I have had experience in retail sales and in working with distributors during several summer jobs. I also achieved a 3.8 GPA in my marketing courses at Duke. Please see my attached résumé.

I can be contacted at (351) 600-1234 or reached via e-mail at johnkt@duke.edu to arrange an interview.

Thank you for your consideration of my qualifications.

Sincerely yours,

John K. Terkel

Easy enough to write, but unlikely to convince a sophisticated sales or marketing manager at Pepsi, and very likely headed for well-deserved oblivion.

You didn't purchase this guide to get bad advice, and our advice is to not attach a resume to your letter—unless it was specifically requested, you are answering an ad, or you are writing to human resources. In these cases, sending a resume with a cover letter is appropriate—but that's not an approach letter. If you do attach a resume to a letter intended to generate an information/referral meeting with a manager, you'll almost certainly be misunderstood. Your letter and resume will go to human resources, probably lacking the valuable recommendation you could have received if you had met with the manager you targeted beforehand.

Instead, write a letter that stands on its own feet and is sufficiently compelling to pique the curiosity and arouse the interest of the reader in doing what you request—which is to meet with you or at least to have a telephone discussion with you. Save the resume for your postmeeting follow-up if you can—by which time you'll know how to revise it to emphasize the points that are important to the recipient.

Outline

The letter, including the recipient's name, title, address, and salutation and your own closing phrase and signature will be not more than a full page in its entirety. Each paragraph should be two or three sentences of ten to 20 words (four sentences at most), typically combined with a short sentence for emphasis and variety.

The following outline should work for nearly every approach letter.

Paragraph I: The Grabber

To entice the reader to read the remainder of the letter

Paragraph II: The Definer

To indicate what the meeting is intended to accomplish and why it will be of mutual interest, while assuring that you are not presuming this to be an interview

Paragraph III: The Convincer

To establish that you are a qualified player worth taking seriously

Paragraph IV: The Concluder

To show your appreciation and business-like follow-up intentions

The Grabber

The purpose of the grabber paragraph is simple enough. You want to entice the recipient to read your letter and consider its message, no more. You are attempting more if you try to make the sale in the first paragraph by opening with such phrases as:

I am a finance major at University of Chicago with a strong interest in the securitization of commercial real estate loans,

or

I would like to discuss with you opportunities at American Express for a human resources–oriented person with strong interpersonal skills,

or

I have admired Wal-Mart's customer service orientation for a long time and believe Wal-Mart to be a company where I could make a real contribution.

Sorry—these look too much like form letters. What's in them to make the reader feel important or interested? You wouldn't try to start a conversation with someone you didn't know in a party situation with a declaration of your own importance—so why do it here?

What, then, does it take to interest your recipient?

How about beginning, instead, with language that might bring about a favorable, warm feeling? Words that show you care enough about the recipient to relate to things that matter to him or her or that are likely to elicit a positive reaction. Words that encourage reading beyond the first paragraph.

There are a number of themes to consider for the grabber:

- **Valid admiration:** for something the person has achieved, advanced, advocated, or attained that is worthy of respect
- **Valid understanding:** of the difficulties, pressures, or challenges the person is likely to be experiencing, based on his or her work agenda
- **Linkage:** shared experience with the same college, home town, interests, community service, or other affiliation
- **Family connection:** connection to or referral from a family member

- **Favorable referral:** from a respected or well-liked third party
- **Curiosity:** as tickled by an unusually apt question you pose, a paradox you frame, or unusual information you have
- **Hospitality:** an appeal to people's natural pride in their community, profession, or organization
- **Humility:** as by reference to good fortune, good mentoring, or other uncharacteristic acknowledgment or disclaimer

Let's go through the various themes one by one and then see how we can construct language to go with them.

Valid admiration. Tell the recipient that you admire something about him or her or that you admire something the person has accomplished. Valid admiration for something real, something that is a source of pride to your recipient, should be heart-warming. It means you've taken the trouble to find out about the person and that you understand something about his or her accomplishments and value. Valid admiration is specific and sincere. This is quite different from flattery, which is simply using words that have no substance for the purpose of, well, flattery.

Valid admiration is:

I'm impressed with the courageous stand you have taken against the short-sightedness of your industry in not approving preventative medical procedures.

Flattery is:

You are well known as a leader in managed care (you assume, because the person has a big title at an HMO).

So, how do you find out what you can validly admire about the person to whom you are writing? Research helps. Maybe you can find a person who knows the individual. Certainly, if you are *referred* to the person, the source of the referral is in a position to know a lot about the person and will tell you—if you ask.

During the course of your information/referral meetings, you will be obtaining referrals to individuals with whom you could usefully meet, as was discussed earlier. When you obtain referrals—and you might well expect to obtain several of them from each information/referral meeting—it is important to learn enough about the person to whom you are referred so you can establish a solid connection.

The information you gain in this manner will help you structure your entire approach letter, the grabber part especially. The following are questions you might ask a referral source about the person to whom you are referred:

- Why, especially, do you suggest that I meet _____?
- What do you particularly respect [admire, like] about this person?
- Can you give me an example of that?
- What do you see as the most important issues this person might be dealing with?
- What can you tell me about this person's style of operation?
- Anything else I should know about this person on a business or personal level?
- What might we have in common?
- How should I make contact—or would you like to arrange that?

It's important, of course, to use your own natural wording, to choose a reasonable number of questions appropriate to the situation, and to not repeat your questions word for word as you obtain multiple referrals.

Valid understanding. Another way to grab the reader's attention is to identify an issue of particular concern to him or her—and, of course, to use this as a basis for explaining why you're the person to help answer this need. As you might imagine, a letter that demonstrates the writer's understanding of your problems can be very compelling. If you know quite a bit about the challenges or dilemmas the person might be facing, and have reason to believe you might be of genuine help, by all means go for it! Here's an example of language successfully used by one individual to secure a special assistant position with a new, highly placed government official:

I admire your courage in defining such a strong agenda for the office you are assuming. Given your background in research management, I'm sure you will use facts as a basis for sorting out the competing economic and technological arguments on everything you will tackle—but where will you find the time to get the facts?

Needless to say, the letter went on to develop this theme and offer a solution. Another example of valid understanding (successfully used to start a job seeker's letter discussing training and change-management issues):

The restructuring you have just announced, from a product line to a geographically focused sales team, must have you thinking about the cross-training that will have to take place.

A less effective example of valid understanding would be:

I'm sure you're very busy these days with all the restructuring that is known to have occurred at your company.

After all, who isn't busy these days?

Linkage. Think about your most recent social experience. Chances are good that if you met someone new, you both searched for some sort of connection—mutual friends, acquaintances, shared college backgrounds, home states, interests. Linkage can be an effective way to grab the reader's attention and establish legitimacy and kinship. More often than not, this will help convince the reader to at least read through the rest of your letter. The questions you ask your referral source can help with this.

Good examples of linkage:

Charlie Jenkins recommended that I write to you, because we apparently have interests in common, including Asian music and Nepal.

We didn't have an opportunity to meet at Yale (I'm just about to graduate in urban planning), but we share a common interest in the development of the city of Baltimore. My interest in

Baltimore began when I learned that my fiancee grew up there, and I've since learned that people from Baltimore can rarely be persuaded to live anywhere else! Subsequently, I've come to love Baltimore and its tradition of hospitality.

Family connection. A variation on linkage is to mention a connection with a family member. An example of family connection would be:

Your son, Mark, recommended that I write to you. Mark and I have shared many debate experiences together, and he points to you as the source of a lot of his skill in advocacy.

In this case, several other themes are being used as well. These include favorable referral (from Mark), linkage (shared interest in debate), valid admiration (reference to Mark giving credit to his father), and curiosity (a father's natural curiosity about his son and his son's friends). Note how the combination of themes makes the two sentences of this grabber so powerful.

Favorable referral. A favorable referral is a recommendation offering positive comments about you from someone the person respects. Why are favorable referrals so much help in making you welcome and creating an initial presumption of your value? Because when making decisions about people or things we have no personal experience with, we tend to rely on the opinions of friends and others we respect.

How do you select a movie to see or a restaurant to try, or choose a professor or a doctor? If you're like most folks, you ask others for their opinion.

If the referring party agrees to make the introduction, great. You can then decide whether a phone call (to establish a time) or a letter (along the lines outlined here) is a more appropriate way to contact the person. If, on the other hand, your referral source leaves the introduction to you, you should write a letter including language similar to this:

Theresa Elliott, your former colleague at Ray-Ban, and I have just met and discussed my research into fashion-industry marketing trends. She thought that my research might be of interest to you. She was impressed with what I had learned and with my linkage of marketing to anthropology and suggested that you would be the ideal person for me to visit next. She obviously respects you a great deal.

Note the combination of favorable referral, curiosity (What has the writer learned that Theresa found so interesting? What is the connection between marketing and anthropology?), and valid admiration mixed with curiosity (What did Theresa say to indicate her respect?). Again, there's power in a combination of themes.

Curiosity. You can pique a person's curiosity, as in the example above, by merely hinting that something might be of interest without disclosing exactly what that something is. Alternatively, you can arouse curiosity by asking a question or stating a paradox:

Why is it that companies in your industry spend an average of $50,000 on establishing a new account, but less than $10,000 on preventing a long-term account from drifting into the hands of a competitor? Perhaps your company is the exception—but then again, maybe not.

You can see how this might stimulate considerable curiosity; it needs only a strong following paragraph (discussed later).

Hospitality. The natives of Hispaniola welcomed Columbus to their shores and gladly traded gold for baubles. Hospitality is a strong human impulse. It's a theme you can use to introduce yourself in a new community or a new field:

Richard Knight gave me your name when he realized that I was eager to relocate to Tucson. He pointed me to your weekly column in the Arizona Daily Star newspaper, and I have now read a number of your commentaries on life in Tucson. They are funny and inviting! I would very much like to meet the author to hear about how things really work in Tucson and to learn who to get to know.

Meeting this columnist became the writer's gateway to meeting the key players in town—people who controlled banking, real estate, and many local companies. A referral's hospitality can be a powerful aid if it's not abused.

Humility. Humility is a rare quality; it is both appealing and underestimated. Isaac Newton is credited with saying that his achievements were reached by standing on the shoulders of giants. Isn't that true of most of us? We so rarely hear due credit given to professors, mentors, or good fortune that humility is a prized attribute. But how to express it?

Martha Booth and I met yesterday to review the work I had done for her about reasons and remedies for the high staff turnover her company has been experiencing. She seemed delighted with the report I prepared, but I must say, it wouldn't have come to much without her mentoring! She felt it would be valuable for me to meet you, given her own experience of finding you helpful and resourceful on her behalf.

So there you have it, a wide variety of inviting themes you can use by themselves— or better, in combination—to create a powerful grabber.

The Definer

You've started your letter with a grabbing opening paragraph that guarantees your reader's attention. The definer comes next.

The definer indicates what the meeting is to be about and why it will be of mutual interest, while assuring the recipient that you are not thinking of the meeting as an interview. You're not explicitly selling your own qualifications yet (that comes in the third paragraph); you're selling the idea of getting together. And the quality of your definer will determine whether you are taken seriously.

This is the part of your letter where you demonstrate your business ability, which can be defined as the ability to invest your resources in collaboration with others in a manner that is mutually fruitful and creates a climate for future association.

Once again, there are a number of appeals that you can employ to advantage. As with creating an effective grabber, if you combine two or more of these ideas, you'll get a more powerful result, such as:

- A reality check on your goals, preferably if there is a clear-cut decision to be made between two or more possibilities

- Obtaining advice on a career or business issue that is well defined and meaningful to you

- Discussion of a subject of mutual interest

- Exploring the possibility of your having capabilities that may be relevant to the person's business

- Asking one or more business questions that illustrate your thoughtfulness

- Requesting assistance in research you are performing that sounds interesting and useful

- Understanding more about the priorities, needs, or culture of the person's organization or profession

You can combine two or more of these objectives, or include others to define the meeting in an intriguing and useful way. You should disclaim (explicitly or implicitly) any intent to make this an interview, while acknowledging that you are seeking an appropriate position.

The following examples will give you a clearer idea of the kind of phrasing to use in the definer.

Continuation of the special assistant grabber (from the "Valid Understanding" section):

I would like to meet with you to discuss whether you would find value in an assistant who could research the backgrounds of the players involved with issues that concern you and investigate the merits of their arguments. All this would be done with an eye toward information that could be useful in your decision-making process. I realize that you may not have such a position defined, but perhaps we could explore the feasibility of creating one. Or perhaps you could suggest other avenues through which I could learn from a dedicated public servant like you and participate in public policy.

Continuation of the Baltimore grabber (from the "Linkage" section):

What I would like to do is pursue my urban planning interests within Baltimore. First, however, I want to get to know the key players in the process that has already made Baltimore such a beautiful place. I would like to learn how you became involved, what some of the key assumptions were and how are they working out, and what your current goals are. Also, if you are willing, I would appreciate some seasoned advice on whom I should meet and how I might position myself to make a useful contribution.

Continuation of the grabber referring to Martha Booth (from the "Humility" section):

Currently, I am expanding on the research I performed with Martha on turnover and retention and would find your advice very helpful. You, in turn, might find my results so far (some of them surprising to both Martha and me) to be of some interest. In particular, I would like to know how your firm regards and deals with this issue, who you see as leaders in thinking about it, and whether this is a fruitful avenue for me to pursue in becoming a staffing professional (and hopefully, one day, a human resources leader like you). Although I am seeking an appropriate entry position, I assure you that I want to meet you regardless of whether such an opportunity now exists with your organization.

Note the explicit disclaimer, which helps justify the meeting even if no position currently exists. In the two previous examples the disclaimer was implicit.

I have a few questions on which I would like your sage counsel. Given my interest in marketing communications, would it be better for me to start in an agency or in a corporate environment? If I go with an agency, what are the pros and cons of large versus small if my intent is to one day achieve a leadership role? If I move into a corporate environment, would it make more sense for me to be part of an in-house creative team or to manage a variety of outside resources? I realize you can't help me with these questions in the abstract, so if you are willing, I would like to show you my creative portfolio and some of the business situations I assumed in creating it. Any feedback you would care to offer would be most welcome—I am a good learner!

Obviously, the writing of a well-organized thinker, and possibly an attractive candidate for hire.

One more for the road:

As you can see from my record below, I have often taken leadership roles. I can sell both ideas and products, and I am fearless (if I've had time to get my facts together) in front of very senior people. Although my academic record doesn't show it, I work very hard, having held a full-time job while attending college. I seek advice and counsel on where I could start to build a career in sales or marketing, in an organization such as yours.

Letting your personality show through, flaws as well as strengths, can be appealing.

The Convincer

Now that you've defined the purpose of the meeting and gained the recipient's interest, it's logical and appropriate to state your credentials. In this paragraph, you should describe what's relevant and promising about what you have done with your life so far. Your recipient will want clues to your character, your potential, and your likability, as well as information on your field or fields of study and academic achievements.

You can convey more than you might think in just a single paragraph. Consider the following examples.

My interests from an early age have been in structural mechanics, and my successes range from winning a County Fair prize for a Lego block bridge at age 12 to winning the Sigma Chi prize for force analysis of the new astrodome in Paris. At M.I.T. I combined engineering and business studies, with the intention of pursuing a career in engineering management. During summer positions at Bechtel and the Battelle Institute I was rated highly by my managers. My overall GPA was 3.75, but what gave me real pride during the past few years was successfully calculating for a Battelle project a system of bridge reinforcement that should substantially reduce both cost and traffic delays when it comes into general use next year.

He talks like an engineering manager, so it's not hard to see him in that role.

The following is a continuation of the final example in the "Definer" section:

I was elected president of my fraternity at Cornell and president of my class at LaVerne High School and was named salesman of the year by the college yearbook committee. I mention these honors because they relate to my true interests. But I take even more pride in having convinced the LaVerne town council to build a skateboard park (over considerable neighborhood objections) and being able to prove that the result was diminished, not increased, vandalism.

It's not hard to see this writer's personality bubbling through:

My interest in journalism began with my father's involvement in politics, but it became a passion when I joined the staff of the Harvard Crimson. *No tougher board of critics could be assembled, but rising to their high standards has invested me with a love of discovery and writing. I've composed pages, run presses, and sold advertising—so publishing must be in my blood. But unlike some who are born to publish, I'm cheerful under the pressures that go with the field, and have often been told that I have leadership talent.*

Your challenge in the convincer paragraph is to craft a presentation of yourself that's both appealing and insightful. As Michelangelo is said to have replied when asked how he knew where to stop as he carved his statue of David, "When David appears, it's time to stop carving."

The Concluder

The final paragraph of the approach letter should express appreciation for the time the recipient has devoted to reading the letter and will devote to meeting with you. It should also discuss setting up a specific time and place for the meeting. Here are some examples of appropriate language:

Thank you for taking the time to read this letter and, hopefully, to meet with me for 20 to 30 minutes at your convenience. I will plan to call you next Tuesday or Wednesday to see when we might get together.

or

I realize that you have many commitments, but I would truly appreciate your spending a little time with me. I'll call in a few days to see what might be a convenient time for you. I plan to come well prepared with some materials I think you will find interesting. Thank you in advance.

or

As I stated above, even a brief meeting with you would be of enormous benefit to my research on innovations in risk management. I would very much appreciate your making a half hour available for a discussion on this topic. I'll check with your office in a few days regarding an appointment.

Note that in each case all the writer requests is a brief meeting. Often, however, the meeting will stretch to an hour or longer if the person is genuinely interested in you—and if you guide the discussion well. Also note that the writers claim responsibility for setting up the meeting. Rarely will the recipient call you, so your prospects for getting a meeting are greatly improved when you take the initiative and make that phone call.

Sample Approach Letter

April 12, 200–
Andrew Kalimian
President
Technical Publishing
200 5th Street
San Mateo, CA 94061

Dear Mr. Kalimian,

I am contacting you on the recommendation of your son Tom's college roommate, Dick Ellsworth. Dick and I serve together on the executive board of the Harvard Crimson, and he has told me of your remarkable success in developing several first-in-their-field trade publications, including Lighting Perspectives, Metal-Forming Monthly, and Flexible Circuits. I am hoping you will be willing to share some of your insights on the publishing industry with me.

I would like to work on the business side of publishing—in both print and electronic media—and eventually become a publisher. Publishing has been in my blood since my preteen experiences delivering papers and selling magazine subscriptions. What I am unclear about is where I should begin—newspapers, trade publications, or Internet publishing. Your perspectives and advice would be invaluable to me. I've done some homework and put together some trend data that I would like to show you. I'd also like to discuss my interpretation of the data, and find out what you think.

By way of personal background, I am a senior at Harvard, graduating with honors in government and economics. This year I was elected to head the Crimson's business office, and we've achieved a $125,000 surplus as of March, the largest in the Crimson's 91-year history. Several of our advertisers have written to thank us for ideas we provided that were particularly effective in reaching the student market here and elsewhere.

I very much hope that you can find time to meet with me, as I know how impressed Dick was with what you had to say when you took Tom and him to dinner recently. I'll call early next week to see what day and time might be convenient for you.

Sincerely yours,

Roger Parker

The Information and Referral Meeting

The networking process, properly executed, proceeds primarily through a series of information and referral meetings.

Information refers to the premise of the meeting, which is to exchange information and obtain advice—not, ostensibly, to interview for a specific job. By defusing the meeting in this way, you make it much easier for people to agree to meet with you. *Referral* signifies the several referrals you are likely to receive from such a meeting. These referrals will be to other people with whom you can discuss your career objectives, qualifications, and your own and the other person's insights, and from whom you can obtain still more referrals. If you pursue all these referrals and continue to conduct meetings where you make a positive impression, you will soon build a sizable network.

Your contacts' purposes in meeting with you, even though they would have turned down a direct request for an interview, may include any of the following:

- They are, in fact, looking for talent but have not yet shaped a specific job description and are therefore not ready to conduct formal interviews.

- They are pleased with the compliments you paid them in your approach letter and are happy to provide you with career advice.

- They do have the kind of knowledge you are seeking and are glad to share it.

- They are intrigued by the homework you have done and think that your research and fresh viewpoint may be worth their attention.

- They respect the person who referred you and consequently feel that you must be worth meeting.

While information and referral meetings are less formal than interviews, it's helpful to have a structure in mind when planning and conducting a meeting. The following simple structure is effective:

1. Opening comments

2. Defining the purpose of the discussion

3. Acknowledgment of the other person's qualifications

4. Brief self-presentation

5. Main discussion (questions, review of your ideas, advice, etc.)

6. Referrals to other resources

7. Statement of appreciation and follow-up actions to be taken

Opening Comments

Opening comments are the remarks that get you started in your conversation—small talk, essentially. With a friend (an A contact), all you need is a transitional sentence from whatever you were discussing up to this point, such as

"Sue, I don't know whether I've told you this, but I'm developing a job campaign, and I'd love to hear your thoughts about it."

or

"Tom, you've done so well at Andersen; I'm wondering if you would share some thoughts on job hunting with me."

When you're meeting with someone less well known to you, such as a B or C contact, you should open with some get-acquainted remarks such as

"I've been looking forward to this meeting, and I certainly appreciate your taking time out of your busy schedule."

or

"I didn't realize until I saw that plaque that you're a Juilliard graduate. I'm in a local wind ensemble, but I envy you the Juilliard experience. Do you still perform?"

You don't want this chit-chat to go on and on—a few minutes, maximum. Its purpose is simply to get the conversation flowing in the right direction.

Purpose of the Discussion

Next you should briefly state why you have started the discussion or arranged the meeting:

"I have a few questions about the strategy I'm following in searching for a job in international trade."

or

"I've been doing some research on acquisitions and mergers in the health care field and would like to hear your thoughts about what I'm finding and what it might mean for my own career planning."

or

"I've had a number of interviews for positions in corporate finance, but so far just one solid offer. I'm interested in your opinion about the offer, as well as whether I can reasonably expect to do better if I stay on the track I've been following."

or

"I'm really excited about e-commerce and about the opportunities it seems to offer for a person strong in both business and creative. I just need some advice on where to focus."

You don't need to go into much detail at this point. Just give a general idea of what you want to talk about.

Two Cautions

1. You asked for an information meeting—don't try to convert it into an interview. If you do, you may be shown the door rather quickly. Stick with the original premise of the meeting. If an opportunity exists, it will come up later in the conversation.

2. Do not state your interest in obtaining referrals as a primary goal. It's okay to say you would also like to learn about other resources that might be helpful. But a blatant request for referrals at this stage, before the meeting is really underway, won't give you an easy shortcut to your contact's Rolodex.

Acknowledgment of the Contact's Qualifications

A simple statement will suffice to both please the person you are seeing and show that the person's knowledge and experience really could be helpful to you. You might say something like:

"Carol, you've always given me such good advice; I feel like you're just the person to talk to now."

or

"Your experience in dealing with corporate finance led me to seek your help in evaluating my experience and figuring out how I should present it."

or

"Terry told me you're probably the single best person I could talk with about my research."

Say just enough, no more. You don't want to embarrass the other person or set off the need for a host of disclaimers. The other person will probably respond to your well-phrased acknowledgment with a statement like, *"I'll be glad to help if I can."*

Brief Presentation

You now have a perfect opportunity to state what you have to offer employers.

The value of a brief, well thought-out presentation is that it captures your experience and strengths, illustrates your accomplishments, and indicates your intended direction; it also quickly establishes your credibility with the other person and makes it easier for that person to help you.

You may feel awkward presenting to friends. In this case, you can just say, *"Maybe I could begin by telling you how I'm describing myself in my campaign and get your comments on how it sounds."* Friends will appreciate your doing this, because they probably won't know or remember all the details of your job qualifications and career plans.

With people who do not know you well, your lead-in for the brief presentation should be more along the lines of, *"It may help if I began by telling you something about my background, my strengths, and my career objectives."*

When the other person gives you the go-ahead, you make the presentation.

You should be making a presentation you have practiced several times, so that you can deliver it conversationally and confidently. There's no need to memorize the words though—you want to focus on the key points, allowing the words to form around them.

While you are presenting, watch the other person's body language for signs of interest and respect (head nodding, smiling, taking notes) or puzzlement (head tilting, eyes deflected). If someone seems puzzled ask, *"Should I explain that?"* or

"Do you have a question?" Normally, however, the other person will respond positively to a well-prepared, brief presentation.

In a later section, we'll take you through preparing a brief presentation step-by-step.

Main Discussion

The main discussion, which you'll reach about 10 minutes into your meeting, revolves around the principal subjects you have come to talk about. Some topics that might be appropriate include:

- Transformations in the role or industry you are interested in
- Changing needs resulting from those transformations
- How your experience might relate to particular jobs
- One or more organizations you could target
- Professional organizations that the person is a member of and that might be useful resources for you
- Research you have done up to this point, some of your preliminary conclusions, and what further investigation might be valuable
- Your campaign strategy and possibly one or more choices you're confronted with

You should come prepared with a statement about each of the two or three topics you wish to introduce, along with two or three key questions about each.

In conducting the discussion, keep it conversational, acknowledge the other person's ideas, and ask follow-up questions. By all means, take notes. At an appropriate time, use a remark such as, *"That sounds really interesting! Who should I talk to to find out more?"* to generate a referral.

If you disagree with a comment or suggestion, don't argue the point. Instead, try to understand it. You might say, *"That surprises me somewhat. Can you give me an example?"*

The main discussion may last anywhere from 10 minutes to 1 hour or more, depending on the other person's availability, interest, and your skill in conducting the conversation. Sometimes you will obtain no referrals, but in more exciting meetings you might receive as many as ten. Even when no referrals are generated, the information, feedback, and ideas you obtain will almost certainly be valuable.

Handling Referrals

You've just received a referral: *"The person you really should talk to about that is Ellen Hargreaves over at Deloitte & Touche."*

While you could just say, "Thank you very much," you should also be asking questions like:

- *"Why does she in particular come to mind?"*
- *"How do you happen to know her?"*
- *"What can you tell me about her background and interests?"*
- *"In what areas do you think she could be especially helpful or would be especially interested in what I have to say?"*

The answers to such questions will enable you to write a better approach letter or make a more effective phone call to the referral, as well as give you background for planning a better information and referral meeting.

Finally, you should ask regarding every referral, *"Would it be best for me to make contact using your name or would you prefer to call her on my behalf?"*

Ending the Meeting

You asked for only a brief meeting, so when 20 or 30 minutes have gone by or your contact begins to show signs of wanting to end the meeting, you should be the one to say something like, *"I know I've taken a bite out of your day, and you've been extremely helpful. I don't want to take more of your time. . . ."* The contact may then acknowledge that it's time to end the meeting or indicate that he or she has more time available.

You'll need to take notes to be able to recall all the points covered during the main discussion and keep track of details on the referrals generated. Before you drive off after the meeting, it's a good idea to write yourself a "parking lot report" that expands on your notes and captures the following:

- What you asked or presented and how it was received
- The responses the contact gave to your questions
- What you learned about the other person
- Anything else you learned
- People you were referred to and what you learned about them
- Any other resource the contact suggested (books, organizations, schools)
- Actions you need to take to complete your research, meet with referrals, pursue any other helpful suggestions, and follow up with the person you just met

You may want to prepare a form with these headings, so you can just fill in the blanks.

Putting It All Together

Review this sample information and referral meeting to see how it all comes together.

You: It's great to meet you, Tom. I realize that your time is valuable, but Charlie Bliss told me there is no one I could speak with who would know more about the business side of telecommunications.

Tom: I'll be glad to help if I can, though I'm not sure I can live up to Charlie's introduction. Charlie has quite a record of his own.

You: Yes, I know. I do appreciate your taking the time. I mainly want to check in with you about some choices I need to make. But first, maybe I can give you a brief picture of myself.

Tom: By all means.

You: I majored in physics at Cornell and am about to complete an MBA at the University of Pennsylvania. My interests and strengths seem to lie on the business side of technology, particularly business development, deal making, and strategic planning. I've had some opportunity to test this through summer internships in the patent department at Bellcore, and this past summer at the venture capital firm of Deboise and Hopkins, which I'm sure you're familiar with.

Tom: Yes, Dick Deboise and I went to Penn together, and we talk now and then.

You: Well, Dick gave me the opportunity to prepare an analysis of a proposed roll-up deal involving two of his portfolio companies, and I think he was pleased with my report—which showed among other things how an extra $12 million could be made through a different means of handling off-shore distribution. And at Bellcore, some of my mining of research notebooks and interviewing of staff members resulted in three patent opportunities that might have gone to waste. One of them could become quite valuable. I found I really liked this kind of creativity, but I'm not sure how best to apply it.

Tom: You seem to have gotten off to an excellent start. Has Dick spoken with you about opportunities at his firm?

You: Yes, he has. And that's one of my questions. Though the money in the venture capital world is attractive, I think I'd like to do something more hands-on. My long-term goal might be to become a general manager of a big telecom business, either on the operational side or manufacturing. But I'm not sure of the best route to take—working through a venture capital firm, joining a Bellcore or a telephone operating company, or jumping into the networking world with a 3Com or a Cisco. What do you think?

Tom: I'm not sure how to advise you. If you were to consider networking, I could introduce you to Paul Peret, who heads up strategic acquisitions at Bay Networks, or John Hooper over at Cisco.

You: I'd be very pleased to meet them both, if possible. Could you tell me a bit more about Paul? . . .

I'd certainly welcome the opportunity to meet John as well. What is his background? . . .

If I went with Dick's organization, I know I could work on a lot of deals. But frankly, Dick isn't in very much, and the partner who seems to run the show appears to be taking the firm in a direction that's not where my interests lie. Are there other venture capital firms that look to you like they might become big players in telecom? What do you think of the TXM organization?

Tom: I know them well, but I believe that Bob Saxon, the top brain in the outfit, has just announced that he's forming a new firm. You might want to give him a call.

You: Thank you. What can you tell me about Bob? . . . May I use your name?

Tom: Certainly. But before you meet with Bob, why don't you give Rod McLean a call. He worked for Bob for several years, and Bob relies a lot on Rod's views.

You: Thank you, I will. What do you think of Cisco's long-term prospects? Will they continue to command the Microsoft-type share in switching, or do you think anyone else can grow enough to be a challenge? . . .

I've already taken a little more of your time than I asked for—I was so absorbed with all the advice and referrals you offered that I lost track. I certainly appreciate your help, and I'll check in with you about how to proceed with Paul and John after you've had time to get in touch with them. And I'll keep you posted on my progress.

Tom: I'm happy to help. You seem to really be on the ball, and you should do very well. Call me any time.

Preparing Your Brief Presentation

Your ability to clearly define yourself and your objectives is one of the principal bases on which interviewers will evaluate you. It's also vital to the success of your information and referral meetings. This section will help you prepare a 2-minute presentation that describes who you are and what you want to do in terms that show you to your best advantage.

Why 2 minutes? Because a shorter presentation won't state your case sufficiently and a longer one is likely to be boring or sound boastful.

Step 1: Develop a Set of Six or More Accomplishments

Begin by listing accomplishments that make you proud (whether or not they have been recognized by others). Give each an easy-to-recall title. It's fine to include accomplishments in a variety of contexts—school, family, community, work experience. All of these areas contribute to defining you and your desirable qualities.

Now develop "action stories" following this outline:

• What were the circumstances that led to your actions?

• What actions did you take?

• What was the outcome of these actions, and what did you learn or demonstrate?

Six is the minimum number of accomplishments you should describe; write up more if possible. If you have employment experience, even part-time, be sure to include accomplishments related to that. These might be goals you met or exceeded, suggestions you made that led to better service or a better product, or difficult situations you handled well. If you did well or overcame obstacles academically, include a story about that. If you led, organized, or redirected any campus activity, that's also an accomplishment worth detailing. Earlier experiences from high school or childhood might be relevant if they reveal aspects of your character that you want to emphasize, but these should not displace stories about your work experience or your academic or extra-curricular achievements.

Developing these stories may take 4 to 6 hours to do well, but you will be rewarded in the form of a better presentation, improved meetings, and impressive answers to interview questions.

Step 2: Determine the Qualities Illustrated

Go over each accomplishment story and identify the three or four attributes, behavioral patterns, or capabilities that were most important to your success. Descriptive phrases will create a clearer picture of the nature and value of your strengths than single words will. For example, say "courage to pursue my idea despite my professor's doubts," rather than simply "courage"; "thinking logically in the face of mass confusion," rather than simply "thinking logically." (See the sample accomplishment stories on the following pages.)

Step 3: Find Themes or Patterns

An easy way to find themes is to make a list of all the qualities you think played a key part in your various accomplishments, preserving the linkage to the accomplishment, as in the following list:

- Listening well to others (community service)
- Defining themes that provided the basis for group consensus (community service)
- Creating an effective action plan (community service)
- Finding common ground between local and national interests (fraternity crusade)
- Organizing actions to be taken into a project plan (fraternity crusade)
- Finding a creative solution that spoke to everyone's interests (fraternity crusade)
- Disciplining myself to work hard even when no one else would help out (orchestra fund-raiser)
- Organizing the activities of others, filling gaps, and eliminating duplication of effort (Save the Lake Day)

Continue doing this until you've listed all the main qualities underlying all your accomplishments. Now look for qualities that are repeated or that bear a close relationship to one another. Write final, succinct statements describing up to four of these qualities. From the list above, you might write:

Listens well and finds a creative consensus that addresses everyone's interests.

or

Organizes action plans and manages their implementation effectively.

What you have now is a set of statements that define your key proven strengths—proven by your documented accomplishments. These strengths are available to serve you in the position you seek.

Accomplishment: Summer Job

Background

I had a summer job my sophomore year testing chemical compounds for protecting metals from corrosion at a research lab in Cambridge. My job was to run the tests, but the compounds had to be synthesized by the staff chemists for me to be able to do this. One day, the distillation column that was crucial to the syntheses cracked, and the testing ground to a halt. It would take 3 weeks to fabricate a new column, but the client was due to review our findings in 2 weeks.

Actions

I was pretty new to chemistry and didn't want to make foolish suggestions. But it seemed to me that it should be possible to simulate the performance of the elaborate distillation column by assembling various pieces of lab equipment that were in standard supply. I came in at night, supposedly to write up my test results, but really to experiment with what I could assemble and find out how it would perform.

Results

By the third evening, I was obtaining 80 percent of the throughput and the same purity level as the custom column. My system used $250 worth of standard components, while the original custom-made column cost $3,000. By running a parallel system, we could far exceed our former output, at much lower cost. My boss was delighted that we could now meet our client's deadline. The custom column order was canceled, and I received a raise in pay.

Qualities Demonstrated

- Determination to ensure that the organization could meet its goals

- Ability to think independently and create a game plan

- Willingness to invest my own time in experimenting and finding an answer to the problem

Accomplishment: Dealing with a Customer Service Problem

Background

I worked in a fabric store during the summer of my freshman year. The store was family owned for many years, but had recently been sold to a new owner. It had many long-term customers, but these relationships seemed less important to the new owner than they had to the previous owners.

One of the long-term customers had begun redecorating her house using specialty fabrics that the store obtained for her at reduced prices. The new owner refused to continue this agreement and wanted to charge higher prices for reorders of the same fabrics to compensate for the "special handling" involved. A difficult situation was brewing, made more critical because of this customer's many connections in town. I wanted to help the woman and keep the store from losing clients, but without crossing the new owner.

Actions

The next time the woman came into the store, I made a point of learning more about her decorating ideas and offered to visit her at her home to see what she had in mind. When I did so, I was able to make several money-saving suggestions that she actually liked better than her original plan.

Results

The woman decided that the "special handling" premium for accommodating her needs was justified by the extra service I provided. The owner thanked me for solving the problem and introduced a decorating service as a new profit line.

Qualities Demonstrated

- Ability to find a way to solve a seemingly irreconcilable problem
- Initiative in pursuing the solution
- Recognition of the importance of client word-of-mouth
- Ability to come up with appealing decorating ideas

Step 4: Pull Together Your 2-Minute Presentation

Now that you've done the analysis, you're ready for the synthesis. Your 2-minute presentation can be organized like this:

30 seconds: a 15-second statement of your background and a 15-second statement of your three or four main strengths

60 seconds: the story, more or less as you have outlined it, of two accomplishments that illustrate these strengths especially well

30 seconds: your career plans, stated in terms of your desire to make a contribution using what you have learned about yourself or what others have said about you

Rather than writing out your presentation word for word, make a bullet-point outline for yourself. This way, each presentation you make will be conversational and can be tailored to the situation.

Practice the presentation, keeping the words and ideas simple enough so that they could be readily grasped by a bright 15- or 16-year-old. As you use and refine your presentation, your delivery, confidence, and success will continue to improve. (See "Brief Presentation: The Wrong Way" and "Brief Presentation: The Right Way," on the following pages.)

The Wrong Way

I grew up in upper Michigan. My Dad was a lineman for the local power company, and my older brother joined the power company, too. I was lucky enough to get a scholarship to Michigan State, where I majored in government, because I like people and thought government would be interesting. I also played soccer.

My grades were pretty good, but I think they would have been better if I hadn't been so involved with running the Sigma Chi fraternity. I was talked into it because my friends said it wouldn't

take much time, but it turned out to be quite a hassle because the national chapter was insisting that we pull up our grade-point averages, and I had to convince them that there were problems with their policy.

Anyway, I got through that, and decided to look for a position in government. It's tough, because I don't have a law degree. Do you have any jobs available? Do you know anyone who does?

Do you find this presentation:

- Boring rather than engaging?
- Irrelevant rather than job-related?
- Disconnected rather than the work of an organized mind?
- Half-hearted rather than enthusiastic?
- Focused on getting something from the listener rather than providing information that makes the listener want to help?

So would anyone you might meet with. Unfortunately, most responses to *"Tell me about yourself"* come out much like the example just illustrated.

The Right Way

I grew up in Michigan, where my father is a power company lineman. With his encouragement, I tried hard to get good grades and succeeded in winning a scholarship to Michigan State. I majored in government because I want to make an impact with my life.

I've been taking on leadership positions since junior high school, when I was class president. I was captain of the soccer team at Michigan State and head of my fraternity, Sigma Chi. I think I listen well to peoples' issues, and I try to find common ground and follow up with an action plan. I also work well with more-senior people.

For example, when the soccer team was in danger of losing much of its away schedule because of a lack of school funding, I organized a parent-sponsorship campaign that raised the $9,000 we needed to carry out the full schedule. And when the Sigma Chi national board *implemented academic rules that I felt would force us to end our major community service project, I won support from the members—who were initially somewhat indifferent—for a protest to the board. That led to a series of discussions and eventually a change in the policy. We received a commendation from the local United Way for our efforts to involve students in the local community.*

I would very much like to find a way to enter government service without necessarily going to law school first. I think I could be of value on Capitol Hill or in an executive department as a congressional aide or a special assistant.

When Information Meetings Turn Into Interviews

It's likely that during some of your information meetings the conversation will turn to a particular position that your contact feels you may be qualified to fill.

Sometimes people will make this explicit. They may ask if you would be interested. They may refer you to someone else for an interview. In these cases, the agenda shifts, and you will want to learn more about the organization's needs, the position, the person you're being referred to, and what your contact will say to that person.

In other situations, the agenda shift may be more subtle. If the position is not yet well defined or if you do not have the specific qualifications that the person had in mind, you may find yourself being interviewed without quite knowing what is going on. After several questions that feel like interview questions, it's a good idea to say something like:

"You seem to have a special interest in my customer-service background. Is this because you feel that it might be important for something you have in mind?"

Such a question should elicit a more open and productive discussion of the potential position.

If you're interested in the position, learn what you can about it, then schedule a follow-up meeting to discuss it (to give yourself time to prepare) and return to the original purpose of your meeting. You might say:

"That certainly sounds like something I'd like to pursue. Could we schedule a meeting for that purpose? I'd like to be sure that today we can cover the issues I came to see you about, if that's all right with you."

If, on the other hand, the position mentioned does not sound appealing, you can politely decline to pursue it:

"I appreciate your telling me about this, and I'm glad you think I would be a good candidate. But it doesn't sound like a great fit for me, because I hope to be in more of a supervisory position, so that I can get a foothold on the management track. Thank you for considering me, though. May I ask you a few more of the questions that I prepared? You've been very helpful already. . . ."

Following Up After Meetings

You've just returned from a wonderful meeting with Frank Carlson. You achieved everything you hoped you would, and then some!

Your 2-minute presentation was received enthusiastically. You asked thought-provoking questions, and Frank gave a ton of useful answers, ideas, and recommendations. He also provided referrals to people he'll introduce you to, or you will arrange to see with his blessing.

You took careful notes during and after the meeting, so you remember the details of what Frank said about the people he's referring you to, as well as the main points of your conversation.

The meeting lasted an hour and 10 minutes, and you're welcome to let him know how things are going. Now it's time to recognize Frank's generosity with a gracious, sincere thank-you note. It's important to send a note within a day or two of conducting the information meeting, for several reasons:

- It's gracious, and it confirms that you are a person who understands and follows business etiquette.
- You can expand on any points that you think might be important to the person and correct any misunderstandings.
- You provide a reminder (by way of expressing appreciation) of promises the person might have made.
- You bring yourself to the person's attention at a point when he or she may have begun to forget about you in the press of business.
- You set the stage for a continuing relationship, which may prove productive down the line.

Writing the Letter

Follow the grabber-definer-convincer-concluder model to structure a good response to Frank:

Grabber

This consists of your appreciation for Frank's time, sage advice, and excellent referrals. You may want to say that your meeting confirmed the glowing recommendation Gail provided when referring you to him. Of course Frank will keep reading to see what else you have to say!

Definer

This is where you paraphrase, comment on, or further develop one or two ideas that were central to your conversation with Frank. You may want to provide further support for an idea, correct a misimpression, or otherwise show that you were paying close attention and appreciate Frank's input (even if you don't necessarily agree with the point he was making).

Convincer

Here, you describe what you have already done or plan to do to arrange meetings with the people Frank referred you to or to follow up on ideas discussed in your meeting with Frank.

Concluder

Close by restating your appreciation (in different words) and your intention to keep him posted.

You can use this simple model as the basis for almost any thank-you note. Later—in 3 weeks or so—you might send a second note. See the sample note below.

Typical Follow-Up Note After Information Meeting

January 30, 200-

Dear Frank,

I can't begin to tell you how valuable I found your insights into the current state of the architectural profession. I remain committed to attending architecture school, but I now realize that it would make sense for me to get some construction management experience under my belt first. That way, I could spend my apprenticeship years more fruitfully, obtain valuable experience, and earn money to finance my schooling.

I'd like to correct a misimpression I may have given you. I have not yet completed my bachelor's degree-in fact, I'm just completing my junior year. But several good architectural schools seem willing to accept students who have completed their junior year with honors.

I really appreciate your referrals to Bill Gault at Bechtel and Robert Woodridge at Granite Construction. And I look forward to meeting Denise Eldridge when you have the opportunity to set that up.

Thank you for your kind words regarding my portfolio. I'll plan to stay in touch as I meet the people you recommended and pursue the course you advised.

Appreciatively,

Bruce Tamarack

Networking Dos and Don'ts

Do

- Fearlessly include on your A list people with whom you have only a slight connection—that's all it takes to start a conversation!

- Organize your networking contacts, your notes, and your follow-up activities.

- Make a plan for what you intend to accomplish and follow it, at least until you can devise a better plan.

- Follow up with everyone, but pay extra attention to those who have been most helpful. These are the people most likely to recommend you when they learn of an opening.

- Persist in your stated goals until a more interesting or promising direction presents itself.

- Believe in and be kind to people. They will respond in kind.

Don't

- Let shyness or fear prevent you from getting started with at least a few friends. Their helpfulness will encourage you to continue.

- Forget to employ the brief presentation, even with friends. It's the result of considerable work on your part and an impressive sales tool.

- Take short-cuts. A written approach letter (or e-mail, where appropriate) will introduce you more effectively than phone calls to people you don't know.

- Give up too easily in arranging meetings or become a nag. Two calls a week is about right, always with the utmost courtesy.

- Allow yourself to become discouraged by anyone's comments, failure to respond, or rejection. There are plenty of other people you have access to, each with an opinion, some information, or an opportunity that may be more helpful.

For even more advice on networking and its role in your job search, check out *Networking Works! The WetFeet Insider Guide to Networking*.

The Interview Process

- Job Specification

- Identifying Potential Candidates

- Screening Candidates

- Interviewing with the Hiring Manager

- Interviewing with Others in the Group

- Panel Interviewing

- Interviewing with the Hiring Manager's Manager

- Interview Detours

As we pointed out in the first chapter, companies use interviews to get to know candidates and to see how they might fit into the workplace. Although better than relying on resumes alone, interviews are an inexact process, carried out differently in different organizations and groups within organizations. There are, however, several basic approaches that you are likely to encounter. Understanding these approaches will help you devise effective interview strategies, increase your confidence, and make a better impression on your interviewers.

The typical hiring process can be broken down into these parts:

- Defining the job specification and pay range
- Identifying potential candidates
- Screening candidates to get a manageable number of people who seem to meet most of the requirements
- Interviewing by the hiring manager
- Interviewing by others who may interact with the new employee
- Selecting the preferred candidate
- Wooing and negotiating with the preferred candidate (and maybe stringing along one or two backup candidates)
- Checking references

If you've done your networking well, you should be able to breeze through some of these steps more easily, or even skip them altogether. For example, if you were at Company X discussing reasons why inventory levels of certain products were at an all-time high, and some of your ideas for reducing inventory seemed worth investigating, you might have defined your own job specification. You wouldn't need to be screened; you might or might not be interviewed by others in the group; and the wooing and negotiating could be completed in a day or two, with or without a reference check.

To present the typical picture, however, we will assume that the process you take part in proceeds through all the steps above. We'll look in detail at each step, and tell you how to handle it to your best advantage (or at least minimize your distress!). Then we'll offer insights that should be helpful throughout the process.

Job Specification

How a job is defined can vary tremendously from company to company and from situation to situation. In some cases the job specification will be developed through careful analysis of the work to be done; the relationships to be established and maintained; and the background, personality, and other characteristics of a successful employee. In other cases, the specification will be much looser.

It will be helpful for you to know as much as possible about the specification—first to determine whether the position interests you, and second, to aid in presenting yourself as a candidate. If you hear about a position through an information meeting, your referral source often will be able to obtain the written specification for you. If you hear of it through a recruiter, he or she usually will be glad to send you a copy of the specification at your request. If the job is posted on the Internet or in an ad, however, the information provided will typically be very brief. You can request the full specification by letter, fax, or e-mail. Simply say that the position looks interesting and you meet the stated qualifications, but you would appreciate a more detailed outline of the responsibilities and a profile of the ideal candidate. You have at least a 50-50 chance of receiving this information.

The obvious advantage to knowing more about the position is that you can better tailor your resume and cover letter to suit the situation.

Identifying Potential Candidates

Campus Recruiting

One source of candidates—generally for larger companies—is on-campus recruiting. Such recruiting is expensive not only in terms of travel and personnel costs, but also in terms of the time invested with the placement office in relationship building, planning and staging recruiting events; obtaining advance information about potential candidates; and paying the fees or donations the institution requires. The fact that a company comes to your campus is an indication that a certain number of past graduates from your institution have been successful in the company.

Recruiters wouldn't bother coming unless they intended to attract and fill their schedule with good candidates and to invite at least one and probably more to go to the next step—the on-site visit. If you obtain an on-campus interview, you are already in the advantageous position of being sought after, rather than seeking. Nevertheless, there are many filters to pass through before you receive a job offer—as you will see.

Advertising, Internet Postings, and Networking

When organizations reach out to find candidates via advertising or Internet postings, dozens and sometimes hundreds of resumes are the result. While some candidates may look appropriate, resumes often proclaim a great deal more than the person has really achieved. Therefore, companies must invest quite a bit of time in screening.

That's why most organizations try to avoid this process and use their network first, identifying potential candidates through employees, friends, and acquaintances. Usually, the manager doing the hiring performs the initial outreach; if this does not produce the right candidate or enough candidates, an on-staff recruiting specialist may become involved. If that turns out not to be fruitful, a recruiting firm may be engaged to find more candidates.

The candidates identified through the networking process usually receive preferential treatment and often proceed directly to an interview with the hiring manager, skipping over some or all of the screening process. They also have the advantage of less competition. This is why it is so important for you to develop your own network of contacts who can recommend you when companies seek candidates via networking.

Screening Candidates

Campus Interviews

If your first interaction with a company is a campus interview, here are some things to keep in mind:

- The interviewers are likely to be junior members of the company, possibly graduates of your school 2 or 3 years out of college. They may know a good deal about you from your academic record and consultations with your professors and the placement office.

- You may interview with one person or a panel.

- Occasionally, a more senior person will participate, typically to see how well you fit with the organization.

- It is clearly to your advantage to read up on the company and ideally to talk with one or two graduates of your school who work for the company. Your placement officer may be able to provide you with names of alums you can contact.

- Campus interviewers operate under tough time constraints (30 to 45 minutes per interview) and try to stick to a predefined format and set of questions. You want to be the exceptional person who shines using their ground rules. You don't want to be the exception who can't fit into their system.

- Legend has it that people interviewed in the lead-off position suffer from the lack of comparison to earlier candidates. Those who are interviewed late in the day may suffer from interviewer fatigue. And some research supports the hypothesis that significantly more candidates are hired from midmorning slots.

Making a Good First Impression

The screening interview is the first impression that rules your destiny. Here's how to make a good one—and how to blow it:

📁 First Impressions

A Good Prospect	Forget About It
Arrives a few minutes early	Arrives late, especially without warning
Neat, well groomed	Sloppy, disheveled, out of breath
Good hygiene	Poor hygiene
Dressed appropriately	Way over- or underdressed, loud attire
Polite, friendly to receptionist	Impatient with receptionist
Good eye contact	Avoids eye contact
Firm handshake	Limp or overpowering handshake
Good posture standing and seated	Slouching posture
Jaw used for speaking	Jaw used for chewing
Confident manner of speaking	Fumbles for words
Easy to hear but not loud	Inaudible, indistinct, or too loud
Illustrates with facial expressions and responsiveness	Impassive, hard to read, difficult to converse with
Good energy, but not boisterous	Dead batteries or hyperactive
Polite phrasing—please; thank you; I'd like that, if you don't mind	Curt phrasing, abrupt or condescending replies to questions
In tune with the interviewer's pace, style of speech, degree of formality	Dissonant with interviewer's pace, style of speech, degree of formality
Answers questions directly or paraphrases well and then responds	Doesn't address questions or gives answers that are not credible
Ends interview with appreciation, enthusiasm, agreement on next steps	Fades out of the interview

Note: You don't have to do everything in the second column to disappear from contention. One or two of these faults can disqualify you, unless you're the CEO's niece or nephew.

A Day in the Life of a Campus Recruiter

8:00   Check out of hotel. Go to placement office to set up for the nine o'clock. Schmooze with placement officer over coffee and pastry to find out more about the candidates on the interview list.

8:45   Check messages. Call airline to reconfirm flight arrangements.

9:00   First candidate interview. Pretty good candidate, but hard to gauge until others have been seen. Put resume in "undecided" pile.

9:30   Second interview. Candidate has high grades, but a condescending attitude. May be spoiled by the attention other companies have paid her. Think I'll pass on this one.

10:00   Third interview. Candidate arrives 7 minutes late, and everything goes downhill after that. Hasn't prepared any statement and is pretty incoherent in describing himself. Another easy one to pass up quickly, allowing time for a restroom break.

10:30   Fourth interview. This one's definitely a winner. Neat appearance. Excellent self-presentation. Really interested, knowledgeable about our company, its products, and its challenges. Good, not overpowering grades, but she was working a part-time job. Definite on-site invite.

11:00   Fifth interview. Another reasonable candidate, except maybe a bit hard to read. I'll have to check references before inviting him—does he really work well with others?

11:30   Sixth interview. Wish I'd scheduled my lunch break sooner. Candidate's answers hard to follow. Doesn't seem organized. I expected better from her grades, but think I'll pass on her. Good, can check messages, then grab a bite.

11:50   Check messages. Darn it. Prime candidate from Cornell turned down offer. Call hiring manager to find out what went wrong. Leave message for the backup candidate. Hope he's still available.

12:30   Quick run to the Student Union for a sandwich.

1:00   Seventh interview. Hard to keep from dozing. Low-energy candidate meets low-energy recruiter. At least I have time to poke my head outside for a breath of fresh air. Only three candidates to go!

1:30   Another good candidate; everything fits, but no outstanding appeal. Not quite up to the 10:30, but number two so far, and the 9:00 looks like number three.

2:00   Nice enough guy, but not really prepared for interviewing, and I don't have the time to coach him. I'll speak to the placement officer and suggest more coaching before he interviews with anyone else.

2:30   Quickly clear that this one wants the sun, moon, and stars—and we're not the ones to be providing them. Anyway, I have a plane to catch, so I'll move out a few minutes early, after saying my good-byes. Two definite invites and one maybe. Okay day's work, but can't wait to get to home base on Friday!

Off-Campus Interviews

Our advice for on-campus interviews applies to other types of screening interviews as well, such as a first interview with a person in human resources, at a job fair, or over the telephone. In these situations, however, there is more variability in format.

A human resources person will usually have an hour available to interview you. But he or she may end the interview much sooner if it is clear that you are not a fit or one definitely worth pursuing. Therefore, you need to be sure that you make a favorable impression right away. This means preparing your opening comments so they are polite and enthusiastic. For example:

"I'm pleased to be here. Your assistant has been very helpful, and I've looked forward to meeting you. I know your time is valuable. Would you like me to tell you a bit about myself, and why I'm so interested in your company?"

When the person assents (they nearly always do), you launch into your 2-minute presentation.

At a job fair, you will normally have much less time than an hour to create an impression that will take you to the next step. You need to be polite, of course, even if you're kept waiting or feel rushed. But the important thing to get across is that you meet the three or four key criteria that the interviewer is using as a screen. You may want to ask about job descriptions on your first pass, go away to consider the criteria, then go back and make your pitch.

In a telephone screening situation, your goal is to get the job description laid out for you before you begin describing your own background or defining your degree of interest. If the recruiter begins by pressing you for answers, just say something like:

"It would probably be a time-saver for both of us if you gave me some idea of the position you are trying to fill, so I can let you know if I would be interested, and if so, answer your questions more relevantly."

Interviewing with the Hiring Manager

When you survive the screening process and move on to meet the hiring manager, you'll receive more details about the open position. The manager will be interested largely in your qualifications, your work output, your work style, and your expectations.

In this as in other interviews, you should find an opportunity to make your 2-minute presentation. Ideally, this will be just after the opening niceties and before the interview proper gets under way—for instance, just as the person is picking up your resume.

You can introduce your presentation with, "It may help if I give you a brief picture of how I see myself. . . ." In most cases, the interviewer will put down your resume, relax, and listen. You've done the hard part, which is to capture who you are in a brief statement. If you've presented it well, you've already built a lot of credibility—and a readiness to let you ask about the requirements of the position you're interviewing for. Knowing about the position and the interviewer's expectations will help to answer questions that the interviewer then asks you.

You can expect to be asked about various details on your resume, depending on the manager's interests and relevance to the work to be done. For example, a sales manager might want to know about your fund-raising work for your college volleyball team, or how you got elected to the student council. A finance manager might be interested in your work as treasurer for your fraternity or sorority. If you've cited summer or part-time jobs, you'll probably be asked what you contributed, what you learned, and if you would work there again.

If you're completing a graduate degree, you might be asked to describe work relating to your thesis, cases, or dissertation.

The hiring manager will probably want to know about your past accomplishments. You've already given considerable thought to these, as part of the work you did in preparing your brief presentation, so you should have several stories in mind and be able to answer this question easily.

Other questions will be designed to bring out information not found on your resume. We'll go over a range of likely questions in this category—and good and bad answers—in the "Interviewing Styles" section of this guide.

If the hiring manager is pleased with your answers, he or she will discuss the open position in greater detail and perhaps begin to sell you on it. The manager may also discuss plans for the future, the other members of the work team, and major projects currently underway.

You may be asked to meet with other members of the team, possibly over the course of 1 or 2 full interviewing days.

What the manager may not remember to do, however, is to brief the other interviewers about who you are and what position you are interviewing to fill. And you may not have a clue about the roles of the various people who will be interviewing you. Now, when you are still meeting with the hiring manager, is the time to ask for an organizational chart and an explanation of mysterious titles such as "new products acceptance" or "process manager." You will also want to ask what the team members will be told about your background and the position. Doing so will remind the hiring manager to do some often-omitted homework and spare you the awkwardness of meeting with an uninformed interviewer.

Follow-Up Note After an Interview

Following an interview with the hiring manager, you should send a thank-you note right away. The note gives you an opportunity to show appreciation for the interviewer's time and your excitement about the opportunity, and to emphasize points in your favor and clarify points where necessary.

When writing a follow-up note after an interview, you can develop the sections this way:

1. **Grabber:** Express appreciation for the time and thoughtfulness of the interviewer.

2. **Definer:** Recite of the goals of the position as you understand them, and the major determinants of success. Express excitement about the challenges and opportunities presented by the position and the prospect of working in the interviewer's group.

3. **Convincer:** Mention, for emphasis, why you feel especially well qualified to fill the position. Correct any misstatements and offer additional evidence of your strengths in areas where you think you might have been perceived as weak.

4. **Concluder:** State your interest in further discussion.

Sample Thank-You Note

August 8, 200–

Dear Elizabeth,

Thank you so much for taking the time to interview me for the position of customer service representative. The opportunity to work in your forward-looking department strongly appeals to me. I enjoy helping people analyze technical problems, whether the solution turns out to be complex or quite simple.

I think my work as circulation supervisor at the Baltimore Sun and cruise manager for Island Student Tours has given me a solid understanding of the importance of good listening, patient analysis, and commitment to follow-through.

What I neglected to mention is my fluency in Spanish, which I think might be a nice extra in working with your clientele. I spent last summer in Chile, which gave me a chance to sharpen my language skills.

I look forward to further discussions with members of your team and the opportunity to meet you again.

Sincerely yours,

Rob McNaught

Interviewing with Others in the Group

If the hiring manager has asked you to meet with others in the work group, you have generated some serious interest. These interviews—ranging from a few to as many as a dozen—require a substantial and expensive investment of company time, in addition to being an ordeal for you. Their purpose is mainly to give the company multiple perspectives on your qualifications and compatibility. While no one vote can get you hired, a strongly voiced objection—especially by an opinion leader—could sink your candidacy.

At least some of the interviewers are likely to be inexperienced at interviewing and will probably spend much of the interview going over your resume. (You should have extra copies on hand, in case the hiring manager forgot to provide them or the interviewer can't find the resume easily.) You will want to ask interviewers about their own role in company and what would be of most interest to them in collaborating with you, if you are the person hired.

Other interviewers may seem to focus on particular areas—such as your educational background, your technical skills, or your thinking about a particular aspect of the job. You should make the best case possible for your qualifications or point of view, but do so without being argumentative. If you disagree with someone's strongly stated position, it is better to try to understand that position than to argue about it. You can always cite your willingness and ability to learn what you don't know. Remember: If you encounter someone who seems to be resisting you, that person may have a friend or other preferred candidate in mind. Your goal isn't necessarily to win over a person like this, but to avoid alienating the person and getting a veto.

The most important thing to the people who are interviewing you is how you would fit in as an everyday member of their work "family." If you seem as if you can take care of your portion of the work, be a congenial colleague, and be helpful to others when appropriate, you will be well regarded.

A thank-you note to each person who interviewed you, varied slightly according to the person and the conversation, is a nice touch. If you send a note to anyone, you need to send one to all. Often, this extra degree of courtesy gets noted and makes the difference in who is selected from among several good candidates. Note: It is important that your follow-up letters arrive within a day or two of your interviews if they are to have a meaningful impact on the selection process.

You should send a thank-you note along these lines to each person who interviewed you—tailored, obviously, to the discussion you had with that person and to what you believe your interaction with the person would be (see George Kilanoa's letter for an example). To accomplish this you need to have taken good notes.

Is it really worthwhile to write *seven* letters (or e-mails) after one sequence of interviews? Very likely each person will note the fact that you took the trouble. If they also realize that each letter is *individual*—and they probably will—you will seem remarkably courteous, savvy, thorough, and hard-working.

Sample Follow-Up Note to Interviewing Team Member

July 22, 200–

Dear Kim,

Thank you for the time you and your associates spent the other day to interview me for the position of customer service quality representative.

You in particular asked some penetrating questions about whether introducing this new position into the customer service group might get in the way of the excellent teamwork that now exists.

I can't be sure of the answer, of course, but you have my commitment on this: If I am the candidate selected, I will consider it a priority to get to know everyone on your team, to work in a style that is sensitive to others, and to request your ideas on how I can get the job done in a way that is compatible with maintaining team spirit.

My experience as president of my college fraternity helped me to understand the importance of listening well to others, and of collaborating with others in order to accomplish tough goals—in the case of my fraternity, conducting a successful fund-raising campaign and overcoming the problems of several members.

I look forward to the possibility of joining your team, and getting to know you better.

Sincerely yours,

George Kilanoa

Panel Interviewing

In some circumstances—especially campus interviews and work-group interviews—you may be interviewed by a panel of people. Each person might take a different focus, or the panel may work well together because the members are a cohesive team. But in some circumstances they won't have decided beforehand who should focus on what, and the interview may become quite chaotic. Members of the panel may compete with each other for airtime for their questions, or one panel member may dominate the questioning to the annoyance of others. You may or may not get time to clarify your answer to one question before another, entirely different question comes sailing your way.

For these reasons, it's especially important in panel interviews to make your brief presentation right up front, so that the group members can focus on what you've had to say about yourself. It's also vital to make sure you (and others on the panel) really understand each question so your answer will be on target and have maximum effect. Ask for clarification if necessary. Also try to remember the panel members' names so that you can address each person by name and perhaps ask any who have not asked a question if they would like to do so.

Take care in panel interviews to include everyone in your discussion. Only one person has asked the question, but they're all listening. You don't need to be obvious about it, but instead of focusing only on the person who asked the question, give at least some attention to the others in the group. If one panel member seems to disagree with or be confused by your response, you might ask—if it seems appropriate—if the person has a comment or a question about what you just said.

In screening interviews, such as campus interviews, or preliminary interviews with human resources people, you should try to stick to the group's preset agenda. But in work-group panel interviews, your objective is to break out of the formal structure into a conversation about the work the group does, the prevailing culture, and the challenges.

If the panel members feel that their first conversation with you was informative and enjoyable, they are likely to support your candidacy.

Interviewing with the Hiring Manager's Manager

First Interview

This interview is often styled as simply a courtesy interview—as if it hardly counted. But beware! A red flag from the hiring manager's boss is essentially a veto. This is a good opportunity to acknowledge the time and efforts of the people you've met and to restate your enthusiasm about working in the organization.

Use this interview to ask about the person's background, ideas for the organization, and view of how your role is important to the organization's success. By all means, use your 2-minute presentation to describe what you bring to the organization, and then relate it to how the boss sees the role.

This person will probably be most concerned with your career aspirations, your fit with the company (more than with the position), and qualities that might someday be important in considering you for promotion. Expect questions along the lines of, *"How do you view a manager's role?" "What was the most difficult challenge you've faced, and how did you deal with it?"* and *"Tell me about how you've handled disagreements."* We'll go over how to answer such questions in the "Interviewing Styles" section of this guide.

Second Interview

You're unlikely to be asked back for a second interview with the hiring manager's manager unless the work group and the hiring manager's boss agree that you're probably the best candidate. Nonetheless, there are likely to be a few unresolved questions, from both the manager's perspective and yours.

There may be one or two areas where another candidate has more to offer than you do—possibly in terms of experience or technical training. You need to be prepared to discuss your proven ability to learn rapidly and your plan to do so in this case.

The manager will want to know about your salary expectations. While you should answer questions about your salary history (making sure to point out that your value should now be greater, given your additional education and experience), you should avoid stating your expectations. You don't want to be the first to name a number, because if the number is too low, you've devalued yourself, and if it's too high, you've disqualified yourself. You can fudge this question by saying that you don't know what the pay range for this position is, but you're sure that the company wants to be fair and compensate you according to your value. The manager may also want to discuss when you can start and what references you can provide (this topic is discussed in the next section).

You, too, have an agenda. You want to know about salary, vacations, bonuses, promotion opportunities, health benefits, and so on. Such information might be volunteered by the eager hiring manager or elicited with some gentle prompting from you. For example, you might say something like this: *"Could you give me a general idea about the compensation range, the vacation policy, and health benefits?"*

Your reaction to the reply should be appreciation for the information, such as, *"Thanks for giving me an idea. [The top end of the range mentioned] is about what I thought it would be."*

You still haven't revealed your own expectations or limited your negotiation potential. And now is not the time to indicate what you would need to accept the offer or to enter into negotiations. The right time for that is after the company has made you an offer.

You will also want to make sure you have a complete picture of the position you'll be filling, find out what the company would expect you to achieve in the first 3 to 6 months, and determine what training and other resources might be available to you. This is the right time for this discussion.

Interview Detours

Interviews can take strange turns. Here are a few favorite stories from the files of interviewers and career experts we consulted:

- Interviewer asks a tall candidate what his dislikes are. "Short people," he says, not realizing that the interviewer is sitting on a cushion to add inches to his height. (Needless to say, no job offer.)

- Interviewer sits across the table from a candidate at a Chinese restaurant. After the candidate has finished his own meal, he reaches across with his chopsticks and begins feeding himself from the interviewer's plate. (Definitely no job offer!)

- Candidate tells interviewer she has heard that she shouldn't accept the first offer she receives. Interviewer asks her how many offers she thinks she should consider before deciding. She says, "Eight." He says, "Call me then. Let's not waste time now." (At this rate she'll never get even one offer.)

- Candidate is invited to the suburban Chicago location of a major corporation and is told to fly in and rent a car. Candidate doesn't reveal that he has no credit card and thus is unable to rent a car. Instead, he hires a cab to take him to the interview and then wait to take him back. Total cab fare is $212, which he bills to the company. (You can be sure he didn't get the job.)

Interviewers aren't the only ones with tales of the bizarre. Check out these real-life stories from job seekers polled by WetFeet:

- An interviewer said that he was looking for someone who had "10 years of experience with Windows 2000." The candidate told him that it might take awhile to find the right candidate, like 6 years.

- During an on-campus interview, the interviewer's cell phone rang and he answered it. He then apologized but left the ringer on. It rang again, he answered again, and this time it was a woman he was trying to get a date with. He spent 3 minutes talking her into going out with him.

- An older female interviewer told a candidate about the thread count of the sheets at the home of a young male co-worker.

- "One interviewer used the 30-minute interview time slot to milk me on my past work experience and my company because he was trying to do a transaction with them. He had absolutely no interest in me as a candidate. It was utterly disgusting behavior on his part."

- A candidate who had put "Fluent in Mandarin" on her resume was interviewed in Mandarin. "I went home and changed it to 'Conversant.'"

Interviewing at Your Best

- Preparing for Interviews

- Dressing for Interviews

- Creating and Using a Portfolio

- Using Your Brief Presentation

- Interviewing Styles

- Dealing with Weird Situations

- Managing Your References

- Interviewing Dos and Don'ts

Interviewing

Preparing for Interviews

We recommend that you do several things before any interview. First, you should learn about career-related issues in your selected field and prepare a 2-minute presentation (discussed in the "Successful Networking" chapter). Other essential preparations are developing key points you wish to make in response to typical interview questions, developing a portfolio, creating a weighted list of must-haves and nice-to-haves in a job, and choosing and briefing your references.

For a specific interview, there are three levels of preparation you can undertake, depending on how much you think you'll want the job.

Level 1—Just the Basics

- Learn about the company from its website, annual report, and your networking sources.
- Identify the company's products and services.
- Learn about the company's financial condition: prosperous, pinched, in trouble?
- Find out where the interview will be, obtain clear directions, and confirm the time. If possible, make a dry run to the location, timing how long it takes and then allowing extra time for possible traffic delays.

Level 2—A Bit More Effort

In addition to the basics:

- Get information about your interviewer from your networking resources, the person's assistant, or someone else inside the company.
- Obtain the job specification, if possible, and think about how it relates to your own experience, education, and accomplishments.

- Research the company's history with the products or services that are relevant to the position you're interviewing for. Is it an industry leader? Did it make or buy the technology? What is the company's competitive edge?

- Learn about the company's culture, if you can, from general business or trade periodicals or from WetFeet's Insider Guides or online Company Interviews and Profiles. A reference librarian can also help you with this research.

Level 3—When You Really Want That Job

Add to the above preparations:

- Some original research on customer needs, what the competition is doing, and how the company is faring in the marketplace.

- Some original ideas that could be beneficial to the company.

Interviewing

Dressing for Interviews

Neatness and cleanliness are the key considerations. If you need a haircut, get one. If your shoes are scuffed, shine them. Your clothes should be neat, clean, and wrinkle-free.

Try to dress as you expect the interviewer to dress; when in doubt, err on the more formal side. Any jewelry you wear should be limited and conservative. (Men should wear none, except for a watch and a wedding ring, if applicable.)

How can you tell what people in the company will be wearing? You can talk with people who work there or who worked there recently. Or you can observe people as they enter the building from the parking lot. Bear in mind that Friday is casual day at many companies and so not a good day to observe typical dress. You won't go wrong if you dress according to the Monday through Thursday norm, even if you happen to be interviewed on a Friday.

Your objective in dressing for an interview is to give people a favorable impression but to avoid having them focus on what you wore.

Dressing to Impress for Men

Casual

You think the interviewer will be wearing slacks and a sport shirt or a blouse or sweater.

Wear slacks and a sport shirt and sweater vest or open-necked dress shirt.

Semiformal

You think the interviewer would wear slacks and a shirt and tie, or a skirt and blouse or a pants suit.

Match what the interviewer will wear—but make the slacks the bottom half of a suit, and bring along a jacket just in case.

Conservative

You think the interviewer will wear a suit, and if a woman, the bottom half will be a skirt rather than pants.

Match what the interviewer will wear. Your suit should be traditional in cut and color (dark gray, navy).

 Dressing to Impress for Women

Casual

You think the interviewer will be wearing slacks and a sport shirt or a blouse or sweater.

Wear tailored pants and blouse or jacket.

Semiformal

You think the interviewer will wear slacks and a shirt and tie, or a skirt and blouse or a pants suit.

Match what the interviewer will wear—but in a fairly conservative style.

Conservative

You think the interviewer will wear a suit, and if a woman, the bottom half will be a skirt rather than pants.

Match what the interviewer will wear. Unless your jacket buttons to the neck, wear a blouse under it, and wear a mid-length skirt.

Interviewing

Creating and Using a Portfolio

Architects have them. Artists have them. Why shouldn't you?

A portfolio is a visual display of your work, which lends itself to storytelling. Portfolios are typically either narrow three-ring notebooks with acetate jackets for each page or loose acetate-jacketed sheets carried in an 8- by 12-inch leather folder. The latter is handy because it also provides space for carrying resumes and a notepad.

Useful portfolio materials include:

- Thank-you or testimonial letters you have received
- Examples of past creative work
- New work outlining important concepts you wish to discuss or results of research you have done

When do you bring out your portfolio? At any point in the interview where you think examples will help you make a point or support your case.

Using Your Brief Presentation

Your brief presentation, if done well, will give you immediate credibility, enabling you to go beyond what most people achieve in a first interview. Therefore, it's important to practice it and use it.

As we have pointed out, you don't want to fight the predefined structure of most screening interviews. Of course, you won't need to if you remember that your 2-minute presentation is a great answer to one of the predictable first questions, usually some variation on "Tell me about yourself."

In interviews with a hiring manager or later interviews with members of the work group, it's usually easy to work in your 2-minute presentation right after the small talk. By doing so, you will establish who you are and what your strengths and goals are within the first 5 to 10 minutes, and the rest of the interview can focus on the position, the company's needs and expectations, and why you believe you are qualified to do the job. If you don't provide this information up front, it's likely that you'll spend much or all of the interview answering questions. The interview will end with you still in contention, perhaps, but in no better position than candidates two, three, and four.

Interviewing Styles

You will probably encounter a variety of approaches to interviewing, and many interviewers will use more than one approach in a single interview. In general, you can expect to be asked about items on your resume that may be unclear or that the interviewer is particularly interested in. This type of questioning, along with questions about your career goals and expectations of your employer, fall under the category we call clarification interviewing. A few interviewers will ask only these kinds of questions—indicating, perhaps, inexperience, lack of interest in learning much about you, or fear of turning you off with more challenging questions.

Usually, however, you will also be asked doubt-resolving questions, which might address why you left your last job, what you see as your greatest weaknesses, and why the job appeals to you. Many interviewers will limit themselves to just clarification and doubt-resolving questions—but some will not.

Interviewers may also use techniques designed to determine how you would operate on the job—such as questioning you about how you have responded to certain types of situations in the past (behavioral interviewing) or how you think you would respond to a given hypothetical situation or set of facts (hypothetical situations and case analysis); putting you into a simulated or real on-the-job situation (audition interviewing); making you uncomfortable to test your reaction to pressure (stress interviewing); or having a psychologist delve into your past experiences, motivations, and influences (psychological interviewing).

The following interview approaches are common:

- **Clarification** questions aim to achieve greater understanding of what you claim in your resume as your education, experience, or accomplishments, as well as your goals and expectations of your manager or the company.

- **Doubt-resolving** questions aim to resolve possible concerns or doubts about your judgment, veracity, behavior, or achievements.

- **Behavioral** questions aim to test whether you have encountered challenges similar to those anticipated and how you handled them.

- **Hypothetical** questions aim to test whether your thinking and judgment are likely to be appropriate for the on-the-job challenges you might be expected to encounter.

- **Case analysis** aims to test whether you can comprehend a complex set of facts, create a framework for analyzing them, and arrive at logical and useful conclusions.

- **Auditioning** aims to witness your actual performance in a simulated or real on-the-job situation.

- **Stress** interviews aim to test your reactions to pressure to see whether you keep your cool or lose it.

- **Psychological** interviews aim to determine the major influences on your reasoning and your emotions, in order to predict how you might perform under a variety of circumstances or management approaches.

Now we'll look in more detail at these interviewing approaches and recommend ways to answer the most common questions in each category.

Clarification Interviewing

The types of questions you are most likely to encounter in this style of interviewing include the following.

"Tell me about yourself."

The perfect opening for your 2-minute presentation! Describe your educational and work background, identify your key strengths and provide a couple of illustrations, and state your intended career direction. Usually, this is the first question asked. If it isn't, you can usually defer answering a different question by saying, *"It may help if I start by providing a bit of background,"* and following with your presentation. Then you can return to the interviewer's question.

"Why would you like to work here?"

Explain what you have learned about the company, highlighting what you find appealing or admirable. Try to be specific—broad generalities sound trite.

Good answer: *"I've researched the leading companies in this industry, and yours seems to be the one that does the best job in terms of customer relations, encouraging risk-taking, and setting tough goals while giving people an idea of how they're doing. That appeals to me."*

This shows you've done some research and are basing your decision on specific criteria.

Bad answer: *"I've heard it's a good company, and I have friends here."*

You don't appear to have done any serious research, and the interviewer may wonder if you're more interested in socializing than in working.

"What are your career goals?"

Focus on the idea that you want to grow professionally, but realize that there may be a variety of opportunities in the company as time goes on. Avoid naming titles—you may shoot too high or too low.

Good answer: *"I've learned from the experiences I described earlier that I enjoy leadership, communication, and negotiation. I'm interested in learning to manage projects, people, and business situations. My goals are to work for a manager I can learn from, to develop on-the-job experience, and to achieve or surpass the goals that are set."*

This links the past and future and shows business awareness and achievement orientation.

Bad answer: *"I haven't set any specific goals, but I know I want to work here."*

If you don't have any goals, how do you know you want to work here? Are you focused on learning, or have you already completed all the learning you intend to do?

"Who is your hero?"

Pick someone—don't answer that you don't have a hero or heroine, because the question is about the traits you value. (If you don't want the job, you might say that no one lives up to your standards.) This should be someone you genuinely admire, and you should make sure to name the traits that give rise to your admiration. Also consider whether the values these traits represent will seem positive to the company. If you say, for example, *"I've always admired Uncle Al because he did whatever it took to pile up a fortune,"* you'll come off as greedy and selfish.

Good answers: *"I've always admired a guy I went to high school with named Joe Curates. He was a paraplegic, injured in an accident when he was 12. He could have been bitter, but he decided that wasn't the kind of life he wanted. He became a fine chess player and trumpet player and was very popular. He taught me the value of managing your attitude and using what resources are available to you."*

"The person who taught me the most was my graduate school mentor. By working with her, I learned how to research and debate scientific questions, work collaboratively, and share the credit. I admire her for her tactfulness, her trusting management style, and her generous recognition of good work."

"Why should I hire you?"

Be prepared to cite the key strengths that you see as necessary to do the job, relating them to your own demonstrated skills, as illustrated in stories you've already told. Then try to name one desirable extra that you provide, such as your enthusiasm, your ability to work long hours when necessary, or your love of learning.

Interviewing

"What are some of your values?"

You can answer this as you would the hero question, if that question hasn't already been asked. Or just name some things you genuinely admire or desire. Examples: a collegial environment, good teamwork, honesty, fairness, willingness to help, trust.

"Do you set goals for yourself?"

Do not say *"No."* Name a situation where you did, and describe what you did to be sure you met them.

Good answer: *"I knew I had to earn at least $4,000 during the summer to pay for my final year at college. My work as an interior decorator's assistant was contingent on her having extra work for me to help with—primarily ordering, sending and paying bills, and other clerical work. By the end of June I had only earned about $1,000. So I got busy and put together a brochure for her that she was able to use at her booth during the Begonia Festival. So much business came in that soon she was sending me out to make sketches and sign up new customers, for which I was paid a bonus. I surpassed my goal on August 10, and earned an extra $1,400."*

"What characteristics would you look for in a good manager?"

Select the elements that are most important to you from the range of traits considered desirable in a manager: honesty, providing clear goals, encouraging resourcefulness, challenging employees, respect, giving feedback, offering recognition, inspiring, caring, being available. (Don't give the whole list, or you'll seem impossible to satisfy.)

"What are your travel limitations?"

If you have limitations, think about these beforehand and come up with ways to work around them as far as possible. And before you jump into telling the interviewer all your limitations (no flying, no trips of more than 2 days, claustrophobia, vegetarian meals only, etc.), find out what the person has in mind in the way of travel. If you can handle the requirements, say so with enthusiasm.

"Tell me about your greatest challenge and how you dealt with it."

This is the perfect entree for telling another of the accomplishment stories you developed while preparing your 2-minute presentation.

"Do you have any more questions?"

Never say no! Keep several good questions in reserve for just this request (more than one, because over the course of the interview the manager may address one or more of them). Some good questions:

"Can you give me an example or two of teamwork in action here?"

"How can I learn what I need to know about the organization's strategic plan?"

"Assuming you hire me, how would you like me to spend my first month here?"

"Have I said anything that causes you concern about my fitting in here?"

And to cap it off, make a final presentation of what you feel you have to offer, and then inquire about how the decision-making process is expected to proceed.

A good closing statement will reiterate the strengths you have that would be most valuable on the job; your enthusiasm for the work; and your desire to become a member of the team. It should go something like this:

"From our discussion, it appears that I could be an excellent sales representative for you. I understand the technology of your product and your competitors' products, I'm good at helping customers find solutions to their systems problems, and people seem to like doing business with me. For my part, I've been impressed with what you've had to say about the organization and your management style. I'd very much like to become a contributing member of your group."

Doubt-Resolving Interviewing

The types of questions you are likely to encounter in this style of interviewing include the following.

"Do you find it difficult to work with some people?"

Indicate that you get along well with people and work hard to understand other points of view. You can name one or two traits that disturb you, but make sure they're not overly broad, and give preference to those that a manager would also find hard to accept—such as dishonesty, incessant talking, or unreliability.

"What are your weaknesses?"

You can say you don't know of any that would prevent your doing an excellent job in the position you are discussing. If pressed, you can turn this into an opportunity to talk about the kind of workplace you hope to enter. You might say that you prefer not to work in an environment where there's no teamwork or where you don't have a sense of why your work matters. Another good answer along those lines, which turns your "weaknesses" into strengths: *"I work better in a team environment, despite the fact that I'm a self-starter and think well independently."*

Bad answer: *"Well, I often oversleep, and I'm a terrible procrastinator."*

You may get a few points for candor, but your interviewer will almost always assume that you're worse than what you say.

If you're asked to name your strengths as well as weaknesses, follow the same principles:

Good answer: *"I think my strengths are my abilities to understand the intent of a project, master the details, and organize and pursue a well-developed project plan. My weakness might be that I can be a little impatient with people who don't keep their commitments, although I'm learning that I get better results by being tactful and persistent in asking questions, rather than making demands."*

Shows coherence and a learning attitude; turns a weakness into another strength.

Decent answer: *"I'm a good detail person. I do what needs to be done, and I get it done on time. I don't know of anything that would prevent my doing a good job."*

Less compelling, but fairly believable.

Bad answer: *"I'm good at numbers, as long as I'm left alone to get the work done. I can't think of any weaknesses."*

Turns a strength into a weakness! Refuses to think about weaknesses or opportunities to learn.

"What would your most recent boss say about you?"

Say that you believe he or she would confirm whatever you have claimed as your strengths or your accomplishments. This is also an excellent opportunity to highlight any praise you received from your boss. Prepare for this sort of question by revisiting your performance reviews and thinking about positive feedback your supervisor gave you.

"Has your work ever been criticized, or have you been told to improve your performance?"

If you say no, be prepared to back it up with a statement such as, *"I've always received excellent reviews."* (And be sure your references will confirm this, or you may lose credibility.) If you can't say this confidently, answer honestly—but it's best to choose a situation in which your idea was criticized, not your behavior. All the better if you can explain why the idea made sense to you.

Good answer: *"I received some criticism when I introduced the idea of a customer satisfaction survey in the placement agency where I worked last year. It wasn't a popular idea with my boss, who feared the results. But I felt that if we were ever to correct our shortfalls, it would be important to know what mattered most to our customers."*

Bad answer: *"I received a lot of criticism from my last boss, who was pretty insecure. When I suggested a customer satisfaction survey to deal with our loss of customers, he flew off the handle. Eventually, with the help of top management, he came around to my point of view."*

Just a bit arrogant sounding, isn't it?

If you do name a problem area, such as a need to organize your work better, be sure to say what you've done to correct it.

Good answer: *"I was assigned to work on several different projects at once, and I had trouble keeping track of things well enough to produce answers right away when people asked for them. When this was pointed out to me, I took a course on organization, got some great ideas, and got everything under control."*

Bad answer: *"I was on probation for being late to work. I got an alarm clock, and now I'm never late—unless I forget to set the clock."*

"What would you do if you were asked to do something that didn't make sense to you?"

Indicate that you would say something like, *"Perhaps I'm missing something, but I'm not immediately seeing why that would be the best way to handle the situation. Could you help me understand?"* If you can, provide an example of how you faced such a situation and successfully resolved it.

Good answer: *"That happened to me when I was working on a cruise ship and the activities director wanted me to shut down the entertainment early to save money. I felt that the several passengers still in the lounge and all the others had paid their fares and deserved their full value. When I realized that I wasn't able to influence her, I took it on myself to find a dignified solution. I explained to the passengers that the band really wanted to rest up for the tremendous party I had planned for the next evening, and I hoped they would plan to be there, because I would see that they got special treatment. All was accepted in good spirits, and my boss was grateful that I handled the situation well."*

Shows resourcefulness in finding a solution that had integrity without undermining management.

Lesser answer: *"My boss asked me to get up on the roof to fix a sign that had been knocked over by a windstorm. I have a fear of heights, told him so, and suggested he call the sign company. He did, and they did a better job of fixing the sign than I could have done myself."*

Although the suggestion was sound, it would be better to have pointed out the hazards involved and to have suggested that the sign company was better equipped to deal with them.

Lesser answer: *"My boss at the newspaper told me to cover a traffic accident nearby. When I reported what I had seen, he asked me to delete the part about the driver being cited for driving while intoxicated, because he was the son of one of the paper's executives. I went along, but didn't feel good about the decision."*

There's no quality being illustrated here except following orders. Better to choose another illustration that allows you to demonstrate skills in creativity, resourcefulness, communication, diplomacy, mediation, or some other valuable attribute.

Bad answer: *"I'd take advantage of the company's open-door policy and make an appointment to see the CEO."*

You also don't want to give an example in which you didn't handle the situation to your boss's liking or in which the result was a discredit to your employer.

"What kinds of work do you find difficult to do?"

Mention things that would run contrary to your values or your employer's best interests.

Good answers: *"I'd find it difficult to promote a product that I knew had flaws that weren't disclosed."*

or

"I wouldn't want to do anything that I thought could harm the company—although, of course, I'd try to be sure I really understood the situation."

Don't say something like, *"I really hate clerical work."* Though that may be true, it makes you sound like a prima donna.

"If you encountered an unreasonable deadline, what would you do?"

Good answer: *"I'd prioritize, then seek out best methods to employ, communicate with the manager about what was going on, and go all out to achieve everything that was agreed to be feasible—and more, if possible."*

Decent answer: *"I'd try to get my manager to set the priorities, because I'd want to be sure the most important work got done."*

Bad answer: *"I'd tell my manager the deadline was impossible to meet and would have to be changed."*

Shows unwillingness to work hard or seek solutions.

"What else should we know about you?"

Here's your final chance for a sales pitch. Don't waste it talking about your pet parakeet or your passion for limericks. This is a good place to talk about some traits that would be valuable in the workplace: You have always been a person others have come to for advice, or people seem to like your ability to deal with stress using humor.

For example you could say, *"I'm the person who goes out at 5 a.m. to get a watermelon when we're pulling an all-nighter."*

If this is the close of your interview, you should use the opportunity to make your closing statement to summarize your qualifications and ability to add value in the position you've been discussing and then inquire about the next steps in the process.

Behavioral Interviewing

Companies have increasingly adopted behavioral interviewing techniques as a core piece of their efforts to screen candidates. What is a behavioral interview? Basically, it's an interview designed to elicit information that will tell the interviewer how you will perform on the job. The principle behind the technique is the belief that the best indicator of future behavior is past behavior. The technique involves asking a series of questions designed to get the candidate to talk about how he or she handled certain situations in the past. For example, if a company has a high-stress environment, the interviewer might ask a candidate to talk about whether she has ever been in a stressful situation in the past. If she says yes, the interviewer would proceed with a line of questions about what she had done in the situation, how it made her feel, how others had responded to her actions, how she relieved the stress of the situation, and so on.

Typically, the interviewer will have determined three or four behavioral characteristics that would be most important for on-the-job success and will have written out a definition of each such characteristic. For example:

- **Good listening:** the ability to listen empathetically to a client's problems, asking appropriate questions and paraphrasing the responses.

- **Written communication:** the ability to capture, in a succinct manner, the most important issues to be resolved, the recommended action plan, and the desired outcomes.

- **Project management:** taking responsibility for organizing tasks, reaching agreement on individual responsibilities and goals, monitoring progress, resolving problems, and reporting on status.

In a behavioral interview, you will be provided with such definitions of desirable characteristics and asked for examples of situations in which you have exhibited those characteristics. Sometimes, after you have provided one example, you will be asked for another, just to test the depth of your experience.

One of the supposed benefits of this technique for employers is that candidates cannot prepare for these questions in advance. However, you can help yourself by anticipating the types of questions you might receive and dredging your memory for examples of past behavior. You may be able to guess at some of the questions by analyzing the job requirements beforehand.

Behavioral interviewing can be a challenge, but preparation will help. You may feel that you didn't have perfect answers to each question—yet be seen as much better suited than the other candidates who didn't even think about behavioral questions. As one swimmer said to the other upon the sighting of a shark: *"Fortunately, I don't have to swim faster than the shark. I only have to swim faster than you."*

The following are examples of behavior-based questions:

- Tell me about a time when you had to work with co-workers from another department on a project. What kind of challenges did you face, and how did you overcome them?

- Have you encountered difficult co-workers? How did you handle that?

- Give me an example of a time when you acted as a team leader. What were some of the issues you had to deal with?

- Describe a difficult customer service interaction and how you handled it.

Hypothetical Situations

The interviewer may also ask you hypothetical questions designed to find out how you would handle a work situation. For example:

"Suppose I asked you to put together a customer focus group relating to a new fashion item we might be introducing next fall. How would you go about it?"

"Suppose I asked you to design a management information system for our regional sales managers. What would your approach be?"

"Suppose you and a coworker had a strong disagreement about the qualifications of a friend she had recommended as a new hire in the department? How would you handle the situation?"

In a real on-the-job situation, you would obviously have more information at hand—or you would be asking more questions. In this situation, you might ask a few questions, then set forth a few reasonable assumptions, which the interviewer may then tailor to what he or she had in mind. This way, you won't find yourself in the deep end of the pool, burdened with a conception that's very different from what the manager may be thinking.

By asking questions and having a dialogue about the assignment, you are also showing the interviewer that you think before you jump into an assignment—and actually giving yourself time to think.

Your next task, having done some thinking, is to describe, step by step, what approach you might take. Then you can add that in a real-life situation you would, of course, look into previous efforts to deal with the same issue, consult with others, and consider other approaches, as appropriate.

One way to prepare for hypothetical questions is to pretend you are the interviewer. What hypothetical questions would you ask? And what would you be looking for in an answer? What the interviewer is seeking in an answer is usually not the conclusion someone else has come to after a month's analysis and contemplation, but a clear and sensible thought process.

Case Interviewing

The case interview is particularly common among management consulting firms, law firms, counseling and social work organizations, police departments, and other organizations that place a premium on understanding your thought process. The case will very likely be the final part of a screening or hiring manager interview.

The case interview consists of presenting you with a typical set of facts that you might encounter in a real-life work situation and observing how you analyze, conclude, and act or recommend actions to be taken. The facts presented can range from a brief snapshot (*"Suppose a client came anxiously into your office, hoping to find a solution to a desperate cash-flow problem caused by an unusually severe seasonal slowdown in his business . . ."*) or an elaborate maze of information including charts, graphs, numbers, and correlations—some relevant and some perhaps not.

Your job is to become the professional in the situation, making further inquiries to clarify the facts, developing and presenting a framework for thinking about the issues, and then working within the framework to come to conclusions.

What do we mean by a framework? In the cash-flow situation stated above, the framework might be an exploration of the bigger picture (*"What has your sales history been over the past 2 years?"*), then a look at potential causes, the testing of hypotheses, and finally consideration of short- and long-term remediation possibilities.

If the case presented requires formulating actions in order to implement a strategy, the framework you use might be a two-by-two matrix, in which you classify possible actions in terms of their relevance to the strategy (high or low) and their difficulty of implementation (high or low). The high-impact, low-difficulty quadrant would be the first area to address.

The interviewer is likely to be more interested in how you explain your assumptions, your reasons for selecting the framework you use, and how you say you would go about operating within that framework than in whether you arrive at a particular predetermined conclusion.

Naturally, if you have access to the particular framework favored by a given organization for dealing with its clients, you will have an edge. You might, for example, find out that consulting firm X always assumes that a prospective client's set of facts is incomplete or distorted in some important way and that the first task is to challenge the would-be client's own assumptions. Discussing the organization with your networking resources will help you formulate an appropriate framework.

(For an in-depth discussion of case interviewing, see WetFeet's *Ace Your Case!* series of books.)

Auditioning

Some employers realize that it is difficult to obtain a full picture of someone's capabilities and behavior in a normal interview. They may, instead, devise a simulation or put you in the real-life role before making a final decision.

For example, the employer might ask a candidate for a training position to make a presentation; a programmer to create a small program; or a telephone salesperson to call an imaginary prospect.

Or the employer might ask you to tackle a short assignment. (Usually these brief tasks can be performed in an hour or less, and you will not be compensated. You should be compensated for longer assignments.)

Such opportunities should be welcomed, because they give both you and the employer a clearer picture of the job requirements and your likely performance. To prepare for a situation in which you might be asked to audition, simply practice your skills. Then approach the audition task as you would if you were a professional on the job.

Note: In situations where other candidates appear to have an edge because of stronger educational qualifications or experience, you might want to suggest an audition. You could gain a lot, and you have very little to lose!

Stress Interviewing

Most commonly used in investment banking, stress interviewing is the deliberate creation of an uncomfortable situation to test how the candidate reacts to pressure. The ethics of this kind of interviewing are questionable, and it is far from certain that the stress created is similar to what would occur on the job. However, it's also true that one person's stress situation is another person's fair, if tough, question.

Some common examples of stress-creating techniques are:

- The interviewer doesn't say anything for the first 5 or 10 minutes of the interview.
- The interviewer is reading the paper when the candidate comes into the room.
- The interviewer asks a tough question right off the bat, without even introducing himself.
- The interviewer challenges your answer by disagreeing with you.
- The interviewer pauses for a long time after listening to your response.
- The interviewer ridicules your background.
- The interviewer takes you into a department meeting with no introduction.

- The interviewer is deliberately very late, then keeps looking at his or her watch.

- The interviewer pretends to fall asleep.

How might you handle such a situation, if you still want the job?

If the interviewer ignores you when you walk in the room, just dive in with something like, *"I'd like to take this opportunity to introduce myself and tell you why I think I'm the right person for this job."* After a long pause, you might say, "Perhaps I didn't make myself clear." Then explain your previous response.

If the manager ridicules your background, you could say, *"Perhaps you expected different qualifications, but these have served me well so far and I intend to continue to build on them."*

If the manager thrusts you into a department meeting without an introduction, just introduce yourself and ask the other people for their names, then explain that you are happy to meet them and learn more about the department.

If the interviewer pretends to fall asleep, write a note saying, *"I enjoyed meeting you,"* put it in front of the interviewer, and rise to leave. Chances are, you'll get the interviewer's full attention.

The important thing, if you're unfortunate enough to encounter this form of interviewing, is to keep your cool, maintain your dignity, and find a way to use the situation to your advantage.

Psychological Interviewing

The thought of the psychological interview strikes fear in the hearts of most people, but if it is done professionally and competently, it need not do so. In responsible hands, the purpose of a psychological interview is to determine whether you are one of the 90 percent of people who are honest and try to do their work well—or if you're someone who might terrorize the office, steal from your employer, or file fraudulent legal claims.

A secondary goal, if you are in the 90 percent majority, might be to identify the type of assignment and management style to which you would respond best.

Most of the questions are likely to focus on your aspirations and your family background, with an effort to find a linkage between the two. Others may deal with topics such as what provides you the greatest satisfaction, what you would like to avoid, and past experiences that you enjoyed or didn't enjoy.

The most important thing to remember if you are to be interviewed by a professional psychologist is to be yourself (you don't want to look like you have something to hide). The second most important thing is not to overly dramatize your family background. If you have 14 siblings, just say you grew up in a large family, unless you're probed further. If you had an abusive parent, focus on the other parent. Don't give the psychologist a lot to feed on in terms of difficulties in your relationships with your family.

In responding to work-related questions, use the types of answers recommended for other forms of interviewing. You want to be as proud and confident as you are in your other interviews. And avoid deception, inconsistencies, nervousness, or anxiety in your answers. You don't want to be one of the 10 percent labeled untrustworthy.

Unfortunately, a few unqualified interviewers may try to play the psychologist role, coming up with such oddball questions as, *"If you were a tree, what kind would it be?"* or *"Picture yourself as a championship athlete. What sport and what position would you play?"*

Give a boring but unchallengeable response. To the first question, oak (stable), maple (well liked), and redwood (long lasting) are great answers. To the second, basketball, tennis, baseball, and golf are fine. Marathoning is a bit iconoclastic, and rugby or ice hockey might suggest latent aggressiveness.

Dealing with Weird Situations

Weird situations might be termed unintentional stress interviews. Following are some examples and suggested responses.

Interviewer Talks Incessantly about Himself

Say you'd like to have the opportunity to learn from a person who has achieved so much. Then ask, *"Where does the hiring process go from here?"* Normally, this will either get the interview back on track or result in the interviewer setting up another interview for you.

Another approach is to ask the person questions that feed his or her need to brag. That may result in you being described as a wonderful listener.

Interviewer Spends Most of the Interview Talking on the Phone

Suggest that you reschedule the interview for a time that would be more convenient and when there would be fewer interruptions. Say something like, *"You seem to have a lot going on just now. Could we find a time to meet when you might have fewer calls, so we can be sure to cover everything that needs discussion?"*

Alternatively, you might peek at your wristwatch—not rudely, but meaningfully.

Interview Is Not for the Job You Came Prepared to Discuss

On recognizing the problem, try to learn the source of the confusion, and retrace your steps to get back to the path of your choice.

Interviewer Seems Drunk or Otherwise Out of It

Excuse yourself as quickly as you can politely do so. Call the next day to reschedule—if you still feel so inclined.

Interviewer Bad-Mouths Co-Workers

This is a good time to listen and not to comment or invite further criticisms. You'll draw your own conclusions as you go further in the interviewing process. But such criticisms made to a newcomer do not bode well for a peaceful workplace! You can also say that you'd like to have the opportunity to meet the department members before drawing any conclusions about them.

How do you handle such situations in general? As with the stress interview, keep your cool, maintain your dignity, and use diplomacy to achieve your goals. But also bear in mind that you are being treated to a preview of coming attractions— at a minimum, you should find out whether such behavior is the norm before signing on as an employee.

Managing Your References

Employers consider references very important—without them, people could claim the most amazing accomplishments on their resumes without fear of discovery. Sometimes they do anyway, despite the possibility of reference checks.

But references are important in other ways as well. They offer opinions on your character, your work habits, your communication skills, your follow-through on commitments, your receptiveness to coaching, and other qualities. These traits are hard to discern from a resume.

You will probably be asked for references before you receive a job offer—sometimes as early as at the screening interview, sometimes when you interview with the hiring manager, and sometimes only when an offer is extended "subject to a satisfactory check of references." It isn't unusual for people to be hired without a reference check, particularly if they come to the organization through a referral, if they've previously held a part-time job at the company, or if the hiring manager is in a hurry.

In any case, your references are valuable to you, and you need to treat them with respect. Obviously, it's a good idea to begin, early in your campaign, by asking potential references for permission to give their names. If they grant it, express your appreciation, offer to send them your resume, and, if possible, discuss your strategy with them by phone or e-mail, if necessary.

You should try to develop a list of five or six references, although you may use only two or three of them in any one situation. These might be former managers, professors, friends of your family who know you well (but not family members), or people who know you through community service. Ministers, rabbis, and the like qualify if they can attest to your service to the community or the congregation or otherwise provide insight into your manner of overcoming obstacles. Try to develop a list of people who can provide various perspectives on your accomplishments, and remember that what hiring managers are trying to assess is how you will perform on the job and interact with your co-workers and supervisors.

Maintaining Goodwill

Because your references are doing you a favor, you don't want to abuse their goodwill. This means you'll want to make sure they're not called too frequently. If they have been called three times already, and you need to use them again, you should call them, thank them for their efforts on your behalf, apologize for any inconvenience, explain the circumstances, and ask whether they are still willing to help. This will help you avoid having your references go flat.

You should also take any steps you can to prevent their overuse in the first place. If you're asked for references early in the interviewing cycle, you can mention who you would use and what they can confirm about you, but say you would prefer that they not be contacted until a later stage in your discussions. Explain that you want to be fair to your references by not having them called too often and that you are having discussions with several organizations.

When the time does come to provide contact information, say that you wish to call the references first to provide them some understanding of the position you are discussing and to introduce the person who is calling.

This approach has multiple advantages for you. It gives you a chance to prime your references. It shows the hiring manager that you treat people with respect. It delays the reference checking until late in the process when the company already has decided you are the right choice. And it indicates that you are giving consideration to several companies and positions—raising your worth as a candidate.

Dealing with Unfavorable References

If you have a reference that you must provide—your most recent manager, for example—but feel that the person may give you a mixed review, have a discussion with that person. Find out what he or she sees as your strengths and weaknesses. Try to show how you are seeking to make the most use of your strengths and are either working on your weaknesses or choosing a path that doesn't rely on them. Ask for the person's own suggestions. It's pretty unusual for a person to give a weak endorsement of someone who is listening to constructive suggestions.

At the same time, it's important for you to prepare a hiring manager to hear an unfavorable reference if you think this may be a problem. By doing so, you get to tell your side of the story, and the manager won't be hearing for the first time that someone thinks you made a mistake or didn't handle your job or a particular situation well. Here's an example:

"There is one reference I'm giving you that may not be as favorable as the others. Let me explain why. When I was hired by Security Services, I was told to notify my supervisor immediately if a dangerous situation seemed to be developing in the mall. I did so after the July Fourth event, when the crowds seemed to be getting thick, and a few troublemakers were starting to stir things up. I immediately told my supervisor of my concerns about the developing situation, but he took a wait-and-see attitude. Later, when trouble broke out, he seemed to want to pin the blame on me for not telling him soon enough. I don't wish to make an issue of it, but I thought you should understand some of the background."

Make the First Call

When you do reach the stage of providing contact information, be sure to call each of the references you have given. Explain to them who might be calling, what the position is, why it relates to your goals, and what you think the person calling might be interested in knowing. You can also request that the reference confirm or emphasize certain characteristics.

A week later, you might call again to ask if your reference received a call. If so, find out what the caller seemed to be interested in, and seek any recommendations your reference might have as far as clarifications you should make with the employer. For example, your reference might indicate that the caller said, "He seems likable, but I'm not sure he's persistent enough to follow through when the going gets tough." The reference might not have been able to address the caller's concern based on what he knew about you, but you—now knowing the concern—could find a way to introduce more evidence regarding your persistence when the going gets tough.

If your references have not received calls after a week, you could check in with the hiring manager to see whether there is anything you could do to make it easier to get through to them—such as determining when they will be available or asking them to call the hiring manager on your behalf.

Bear in mind that the hiring manager may already be satisfied that you are the right person. On the other hand, the manager may be having discussions with another candidate and holding you in reserve. Either way, your thoughtful persistence will leave a positive impression.

Interviewing Dos and Don'ts

Do

- Prepare thoroughly in advance.

- Prepare your list of references, obtain their permission, and seek their advice.

- Use your brief presentation early in your interviews to gain immediate credibility, and then move directly to a discussion of the position.

- Reserve discussion of expected salary and benefits until the employer starts mentioning numbers or makes an offer.

- Ask for a definition of the position that includes the responsibilities and performance expectations.

- Make sure you understand questions before answering them.

- Be gracious and polite in your dealings with everyone.

Don't

- Jump to conclusions about a position until you've met the relevant people. Many positions that sound good will disappoint—and vice versa.

- Allow yourself too little time to get to the interview. You won't shine as a late-arriving, hard-breathing, anxious candidate. If lateness is unavoidable, call ahead to reset the time or reschedule the appointment.

- Go into interviews without thinking through answers to likely questions.

- Assume that you're the only candidate until you've received a written offer—and be aware that written offers can be withdrawn if you become difficult to deal with.

- Get discouraged if you get turned down. Write a gracious thank-you note, ask for a chance to get feedback, and try to set up another discussion with the manager. Then move on with your campaign. Fortune will soon smile on you!

Getting the Best Offer

- Clarifying Offers

- Weighing Your Own Requirements

- Negotiating with the Right Person

- Dealing with Multiple Opportunities

When the hiring manager has decided that you are probably the best candidate for the position, you will start to see some buy signs. These might include the following:

- Enthusiastic discussion of the organization, the department's exciting goals, the fine opportunities for you, the wonderful colleagues, the great chances for promotion, and so on

- Eager inquiry about your views so far, your salary needs or expectations, any other positions you might be considering, and when you might be able to start

- Interest in setting up a meeting with the boss or other senior people

- Providing names of people you might wish to speak with about the organization

- Asking for your references

Clarifying Offers

While it's gratifying to be treated with such respect, now is not the time to throw caution to the wind. You still want to make sure this is the right job for you. You still want to preserve your bargaining position. And you still want to establish the expectations, goals, and responsibilities of your new role.

You want the company to make an offer first. If you volunteer your expectations first, you may be naming a salary or other requirements (e.g., flex time, a commission, or a title) that remove you from consideration, even though you might have found their offer acceptable. Or you may be asking for less than they were willing to give. In that case, you'll not only shortchange yourself, but may even cause them to think that you aren't quite as valuable as they had believed.

So, get them to define the position, the responsibilities, and the compensation first, preferably in writing. Then do your negotiations.

Suppose you find the offer totally acceptable? You'll still want to do some negotiating, even if you decide to accept the original terms. This is to prevent buyer's remorse—maybe you've been offered too much! Maybe the salary review should be delayed beyond the normal 6 months to compensate!

Weighing Your Own Requirements

Earlier, we recommended that you prepare a weighted list of must-haves and nice-to-haves as part of your preparation for interviewing. Now's the time to refer to that list. How does this job measure up? Is it a 95, an 85, or maybe a dog of a 35?

If it's a dog, why are you considering it? Something better should come along soon, if you keep working at it in the ways we recommend. If it's a 95, why keep looking? Nothing's perfect, and very little is 95! But if the job rates somewhere in between, you have a tougher decision.

Perhaps you have one offer, several prospects, and a few more distant possibilities. Try using your rating scale to see what's good and not so good about each. Then try to clarify whether the apparent differences are real and whether you have omitted any factors that are important to you, but are not named as one of your must-haves or nice-to-haves.

If you're considering several positions that are within a few points of each other and well into the 80s or 90s, there probably is no wrong choice. Just develop all these opportunities to the best of your ability. You may find that some of what's attractive about one position (tuition reimbursements, moving allowances, sign-on bonuses, etc.) can be negotiated for another position.

Negotiating with the Right Person

You may receive your offer from human resources or a recruiter, rather than from the hiring manager. But it's to your advantage to negotiate with the hiring manager. Why? Because the hiring manager has the most to give (he or she has a budget) and the most to gain (namely, his or her own goals). Therefore, this is the person who will try hardest on your behalf and who will have more clout than someone in human resources.

How do you arrange to do this? Once you have a written offer, say that you need to discuss the role and responsibilities with the hiring manager before you can make a decision. After you have done so, and you are both satisfied, you can move into a discussion and negotiation of the actual offer.

When you have a written offer in hand and you've negotiated the terms of your agreement, all you need to do is add amending paragraphs at the end to cover whatever revisions or additions you've agreed to, and sign and date the amendments. If you also make corrections to the original language, initial and date each such change, and write "accepted as modified" at the bottom. Alternatively, the manager may prefer to incorporate the revised terms into a new letter.

One thing to remember: A successful negotiation leaves both parties satisfied. You have to live in the organization. You don't want a manager who resents you because you enjoy privileges that will cause grief with others.

Dealing with Multiple Opportunities

You may find yourself in a position where you have several opportunities, and perhaps the most desirable one is not yet a full offer. In this situation, you'll want to delay offers A and B so you can look at offer C if and when it comes through. What can you do?

You can certainly present the situation to the hiring manager in charge of offer C and see whether you can get some indication of his or her interest. If it's strong, perhaps he or she can accelerate the process. You can reasonably delay things by asking for offer A in writing, having a follow-up discussion with that hiring manager, and perhaps requesting a meeting with the manager's boss. And finally, of course, you can ask for a few days to a week or so to choose between two or three very appealing situations.

Of course, if you push it too far, be aware that the hiring manager may seek to develop a backup candidate—and may decide that the backup candidate is preferable. The hazard here is that the backup candidate has fresh appeal, while too much haggling with you may have tarnished your luster.

So you could lose out. Hopefully you'll realize this and gamble with time only if you have a good backup situation in the form of other prospects.

You need to weigh these factors—and live with your decision. That's business for you: making decisions with incomplete information!

My Job Requirements

Factors to Consider	Ideal (%)	Job A (%)	Job B (%)	Job C (%)
Essential	**(75%)**			
Learning and growth opportunity	25	20	25	22
Great colleagues	15	10	14	9
Pioneering work	15	5	11	12
Travel/adventure	10	3	7	8
Compensation	10	8	5	7
Nice to Have	**(25%)**			
Reasonable work hours	9	7	3	4
Nice boss	9	9	5	8
Recognition	5	2	4	4
Medical benefits	2	2	0	2
Total	**100%**	**66**	**74**	**76**

Final Steps

- Wrapping Up a Successful Search

- Handling a Turn-Down

- Additional Resources

Wrapping Up a Successful Search

You've signed off on your amended offer letter and selected a starting date. Congratulations!

First, you need to immediately advise any employers who have made offers or are actively considering your candidacy that you have decided to accept another position. If they invest additional time or money in your candidacy, only to find out that you began working elsewhere 2 weeks ago, your thoughtlessness will definitely cool any future relationships with those companies. When informing employers of your decision, tell them that it was difficult because their organization is excellent in so many ways, but you needed to choose the best overall fit (or future prospects) for you. A voice-mail message will suffice if the key person can't be easily reached. Timeliness is the priority once you've made a firm commitment.

Second, you need to thank your references—you'll probably need them again some day. Tell them how happy you are to advise them of your new position, and describe what you will be doing. Thank them for their part in making it possible. A written note would be nice, but at least a phone conversation (not just a voice-mail message) is due.

Finally, you need to phone or write, as appropriate, every person who was kind enough to provide time, advice, and referrals during the course of your campaign. They're now part of your network, and you are part of theirs—keep it alive. They'll appreciate your professionalism and courtesy and be glad to help you again in the future.

Handling a Turn-Down

We'd be remiss if we didn't acknowledge that in every job search, a little rain must fall. Not every interview will lead to a job offer. Sometimes you won't want a job offer from a given employer. And sometimes you will, and it won't materialize. In those cases, there are a couple of things you can do to turn those lemons into lemonade.

Seek Feedback

Let's suppose you've been interviewing for your dream job, an international market-research position at a hot athletic equipment company. Your role would be to run focus groups, show video clips of ad mock-ups featuring various sports idols, and test reactions to the ad concepts. The job would make excellent use of your language skills in French and German, appeal to your interest in psychology, and provide travel opportunities and a liberal expense account. You know that at least 20 people have interviewed for this position, but you've handled yourself well, been complimented on your presentation, and been given reason to believe that an offer is forthcoming. You await the mail each day with great anticipation.

Soon, the letter comes—but the contents are crushing.

Dear Julie, it goes, *Thank you for taking part in the interview process for the market-research position in the International Marketing department. Your credentials are impressive and you presented yourself well. Unfortunately, we have decided to hire another well-qualified individual for this position and therefore cannot make an offer to you at this time. We will keep your resume on file.*

What would you do in this circumstance, if you were Julie? Would you cry? (Possibly.) Would you whine to others? (Probably.) Would you try to get on with your job search and just try to forget about your disappointment? (Maybe.)

No—you do the smart thing and write Ellen the following letter.

 Sample Follow-Up Letter

November 12, 200–

Ellen Reed
Manager, International Marketing
Vega Sports Company
335 Seventh Ave., Third Floor
New York, NY 10001

Dear Ellen,

Thank you so much for the opportunity to interview with you and the members of your international marketing team. Everyone seems committed, intelligent, and enthusiastic. I learned a great deal meeting with them and with you—and was hopeful that I might be able to become a member of your group and a key contributor in helping you reach your goals.

As I understood the position, it required the ability to approach strangers, to quickly build rapport, and to conduct meetings that obtain legitimate and useful information while giving participants a positive impression of your organization. It is essential to seek out statistically valid participation and to be alert to between-the-lines information—something that requires sensitivity and fluency in the language spoken by the focus-group participants. If done effectively, I'm sure the research will make your European advertising even more successful than it is today. I'm confident that I could have delivered exactly what you need, but I also understand that you have made a thoughtful decision in selecting another person.

What I would truly appreciate would be the opportunity to meet with you again to obtain your valuable suggestions regarding my presentation and my ongoing campaign to secure a position in market research where I can use my existing skills, gain valuable experience, and make a real contribution.

May I call you in a few days to see if this would be possible? I would truly appreciate it, as you seem to have such a fine perspective on what it takes to succeed in international marketing today.

Sincerely yours,

Julie Machoute

What does such a letter say about Julie? Most people would see Julie as:

- Polite and gracious, even when disappointed
- Accepting of Ellen's decision (or at least not argumentative)
- Persistent in striving for her goals
- Open to suggestions
- Eager to learn from someone she respects
- Knowledgeable about what the position required
- Confident of her own abilities and yet willing to learn
- Articulate in expressing herself

All of these attributes would theoretically make her a valuable employee, especially in a high-profile marketing position. Unfortunately, the position is already gone! Why bother? Here's why:

Shortly after receiving Julie's letter, Ellen gets an unpleasant call. The call begins: *"Ellen, this is a very difficult call for me to make. As it happens . . ."* The candidate hired instead of Julie has just learned of another opportunity, the perfect opportunity, the opportunity that she just couldn't turn down. Or perhaps her current boss made her a counter-offer that was too good to be true. Bottom line, she won't be coming to work for Ellen.

Now Ellen really is on the spot. Her market research is due to begin next week and she has no one to send. Her options? Begin interviewing all over again or try to figure out which of the other 19 candidates she might look at again after having turned them all down. No one but Julie wrote a thank-you note after being turned down for the job or made it so easy for Ellen to get back in touch. All Ellen has to do is pick up the phone and agree to see Julie again—and tomorrow would actually be the most convenient day. By Wednesday night, guess who's on her way to Europe?

Is this for real? You can count on it. According to a survey of career counselors, one-third of well-written thank-you notes after a job turn-down have resulted in either a job offer into the same position, a lead into another position with the same company, or a lead on a position elsewhere, usually with a laudatory introduction from the person making the referral.

The sample letter also illustrates a key principle in the hiring process: People tend to hire the individuals they *like* the most, people they feel will *fit in*, and those who *won't let them down in a crisis*. If you can somehow project those qualities, you can win positions over individuals who may have some advantage in knowledge or experience. A follow-up note like Julie's is one of a number of ways to demonstrate such qualities.

Submit a Proposal for Services

If the above scenario doesn't quite describe your position, consider whether the following scenario is more apt: Suppose you do not quite fit the position the company is currently trying to fill. However, you see a need that exists outside the scope of any current role at the company. You've worked to define the nature and importance of this need, and feel that you have the resources to address it.

Why not submit a proposal letter? Here's an example:

Sample Proposal for Services Letter

July 22, 200–

Dear Leona,

Thank you for the opportunity to interview for the position of research administrator in your research services organization. I think we came to the same conclusion—that the position is not a great fit for me, as much as I would like to work for you.

However, I think we both noted that documentation of discoveries is a real need that is not being fully addressed. As a result, Vee-Trex stands to lose priority and patentability on some of its expensively acquired results.

Documentation of discoveries holds compelling interest for me, and I think I'm quite well prepared to handle such a role. I was trained as a chemist, as you know, but you perhaps did not know that I also wrote the science column for my college newspaper, on my own initiative. I have some ideas about how a documentation of discoveries position might function within your organization. Obviously, we would need to discuss them in depth before you could consider creating the position.

I will plan to call you in a few days to see when we can get together.

Sincerely yours,

Susan Rosenburg

Additional Resources

WetFeet publishes a number of Insider Guides to help you with your job search.

Ace Your Case! Series

Like it or not, if you're planning to land a job with a consulting firm, you will have to master the dreaded case interview. Fortunately for you and thousands of wannabe consultants before you, the interview experts at WetFeet developed the *Ace Your Case!* series. Drawing on conversations with those who have braved the consulting interview gauntlet, the books in this series outline common question types, offer tips on how to attack each, and present practice questions followed by thorough examples of good and bad answers.

Ace Your Interview!

This book draws on the advice of interviewing and hiring experts to bring you the latest wisdom and practical advice for the interviewing process—from phone screens to behavioral interviews to panel interviews and beyond. Learn how to conduct focused pre-interview research to determine what employers are looking for and how to give it to them.

Beat the Street: Investment Banking Interviews

WetFeet's Insider Guide to investment banking interviews outlines the process in detail. You'll learn how to value a company; about the power plays that take place during I-banking interviews; how to gain the respect and trust of the recruiters on the other side of the table; and how to prepare for your interviews in corporate finance, research, sales, and trading.

Killer Cover Letters and Resumes

Everything you need to catch the eye of a potential employer, with plenty of sample before-and-after resumes and cover letters, recruiters' pet peeves, and more! By Rosanne Lurie.

Negotiating Your Salary and Perks

For in-depth advice on how to negotiate the compensation and benefits package you deserve, turn to this Insider Guide. You'll learn how to build your bargaining power and stand out as the candidate for the job; how to present your case to get a better job—and, of course, more money; how to discuss your salary history without limiting your earning power; and how to spot hiring managers' own negotiating tactics—and overcome them.

Networking Works!

Most job vacancies are filled well before a job description is posted. How do people know about these secret openings? Networking! This book will show you how to network effectively, even if you don't know where to start. Learn to tap and expand on your existing network, read about alternative means of networking, using online and community resources, and master the subtle art of small talk.

About the Author

Robert A. Fish, PhD, is an expert on the skills needed to climb the corporate ladder. Over the past 20 years he has personally counseled thousands of executives, managers, and professionals on marketing their talents.

Rob's own career demonstrates his expertise in personal marketing. He founded and heads the consulting firm SageWorks, which provides strategic and marketing advice to companies seeking rapid growth and better bottom lines. Previously, he cofounded Right Management Consultants, Inc., the world's largest outplacement, career-management, and career-transition firm. While there, he developed many of the company's written materials and training programs, and opened offices in several locations.

Earlier, Rob founded and was CEO of a software company that developed decision-analysis products for airlines. And during the Kennedy administration he headed up government studies of major technology issues, such as development of a supersonic transport, satellites for communications and navigation, and remote sensing. He earned his PhD in astrophysics at the University of Chicago and is a graduate of Harvard.

WETFEET'S INSIDER GUIDE SERIES

JOB SEARCH GUIDES

Getting Your Ideal Internship

Job Hunting A to Z: Landing the Job You Want

Killer Consulting Resumes

Killer Investment Banking Resumes

Killer Cover Letters & Resumes

Negotiating Your Salary & Perks

Networking Works!

INTERVIEW GUIDES

Ace Your Case: Consulting Interviews

Ace Your Case II: 15 More Consulting Cases

Ace Your Case III: Practice Makes Perfect

Ace Your Case IV: The Latest & Greatest

Ace Your Case V: Return to the Case Interview

Ace Your Interview!

Beat the Street: Investment Banking Interviews

Beat the Street II: I-Banking Interview Practice Guide

CAREER & INDUSTRY GUIDES

Careers in Accounting

Careers in Advertising & Public Relations

Careers in Asset Management & Retail Brokerage

Careers in Biotech & Pharmaceuticals

Careers in Brand Management

Careers in Consumer Products

Careers in Entertainment & Sports

Careers in Human Resources

Careers in Information Technology

Careers in Investment Banking

Careers in Management Consulting

Careers in Manufacturing

Careers in Marketing & Market Research

Careers in Nonprofits & Government Agencies

Careers in Real Estate

Careers in Supply Chain Management

Careers in Venture Capital

Consulting for PhDs, Doctors & Lawyers

Industries & Careers for MBAs

Industries & Careers for Undergrads

COMPANY GUIDES

Accenture

Bain & Company

Boston Consulting Group

Booz Allen Hamilton

Citigroup's Corporate & Investment Bank

Credit Suisse First Boston

Deloitte Consulting

Goldman Sachs Group

J.P. Morgan Chase & Company

Lehman Brothers

McKinsey & Company

Merrill Lynch

Morgan Stanley

25 Top Consulting Firms

Top 20 Biotechnology & Pharmaceuticals Firms

Top 25 Financial Services Firms